# HERE'S WHAT PEOPLE ARE SAYING ABOUT "10 INSIDER SECRETS TO JOB HUNTING SUCCESS!"

## Celebrity Experts!

"Excellent . . . Outstanding . . . The best job hunting book I have ever read!"

—Les Brown, Author, Speaker, Radio and Television Celebrity

"Whether you are job hunting for the first time or have years of work experience, this book gives you the most up-to-date and essential tips and techniques you need to get the job you want . . . even in tough times!"

—Brian Tracy, World-Renowned Author, Speaker, and Consultant

"Great strategies to crush the fears associated with finding a job and practical ways to release the power to get the job you really want."

—Karen S. Hinds, Professional Speaker,
Author of *Get Along, Get Ahead*: *101 Courtesies for the New Workplace*

## Career Experts and Job Recruiters!

"Many job seekers think today's point and click Internet technology has made job hunting easier. Not so! It has made it more competitive and many of the old rules still apply. A recruiter needs to select the best candidates. Bermont gives you a clear, step-by-step approach that will separate you from the competition and increase your opportunities for successful job placement."

—Anita Grant, Technical Recruiter, Management Recruiters, Inc.

"If job hunting were a movie, this book would be the perfect script!"

—Carole Nicolaides, Executive Coach and Founder, Progressive Leadership
(www.progressiveleadership.com)

"Mr. Bermont has written an incredibly comprehensive, informative and effective tool that every job-seeker should have. The tips and 'insider' advice he gives show tremendous insight into job hunting, and should give anyone who reads his book a huge advantage in this ultra-competitive job market."

—Frazer Donaldson, President, LionSearch, Inc.
(www.lionsearch.net), Information Technology Search Professionals

"This is an excellent book for those wanting to get ahead in the job market. Bermont goes above and beyond any information that one needs in order to get the right opportunity. I highly recommend reading and following through on all his suggestions."

—Natalie Shuler, Technical Recruitment Consultant

## Hiring Managers!

"Too many writers try to educate others without proven success for themselves. Bermont gives readers real business experience, not theory!"

—Bryan West, Director of Consumer Business, APC Corporation

"Unbelievable . . . this book gives away so many secrets it should be illegal! This book is worth its weight in gold!"

—Nat Hanan, Director, Enterprise Sales, ADC Telecommunications

"Bermont's advice is real-life and right on the money!"

—Steven Weintraub, President, Pre-Paid Communications

"Great book . . . not only is it full of terrific advice . . . this book is actually fun to read!"

—Paula Maslov, Accounting Manager, Friendship Village

## Job Hunters!

"I always wanted to work overseas. The information in this book helped me land the job of my dreams in Koyoto, Japan!"

—Lucas Zastrow, Iowa City, Iowa

"My only regret was that I didn't read this book sooner. Bermont's secrets gave me the confidence and direction I needed. After reading this book, I landed a fantastic job!"

—Kenneth Weine, Evanston, IL

"This is the best job hunting book I have ever read. It really is 8 books in 1!"

—Esther Taylor, Winnipeg, Manitoba

"Comprehensive, practical and easy-to-follow! This book shows how to make the right career move and how to be successful in job hunting!"

—Kirill Bodrashov, Budapest, Hungary

# 10 *INSIDER* SECRETS TO JOB HUNTING SUCCESS!

**EVERYTHING YOU NEED TO GET THE JOB YOU WANT IN 24 HOURS—OR LESS!**

**10STEP** Publications

CHICAGO

**Copyright © 2002 by 10 Step Publications**

1151 N. State Parkway, Suite #253, Chicago, IL 60610

www.10InsiderSecretsToJobHuntingSuccess.com or www.10StepPublications.com

1(888)894-6400

Printed in the United States of America

ISBN: 0-9713569-0-4

LCCN: 2001134108

Cover photo: John Reilly
Cover design: The Floating Gallery
Interior design: The Floating Gallery
Book Consultant/Editor: The Floating Gallery

Bermont, Todd, 1964
10 Insider Secrets To Job Hunting Success!
Everything You Need to Get The Job You Want in 24 Hours—or Less!
Todd Bermont. - - 1st ed.

# AUTHOR'S NOTE

Dear Reader,

All of the information contained in this book is based on my real life job hiring, job hunting and job interviewing experiences.

This book is written to give you a complete step-by-step guide on how to get a job in any economy. It is my intention to offer you an entirely new perspective on job hunting . . . one that comes from both sides of the interview desk.

This book is designed to provide you with an unfair advantage when searching for a job, and to help you have FUN with the process. It is my sincere hope that the secrets, strategies, tips and techniques you find here are beneficial not only in your job hunt, but also in your personal life.

Please enjoy!


Todd L. Bermont

## DEDICATION

**D**edicated to my mother, Margot Bermont, and my wonderful family. Their tremendous love and support has given me the courage to follow a dream. I will always remember the advice my mother gave me in her final days . . .

**"I would rather regret what I did do than what I didn't do!" —Margot Bermont**

Living by those words has changed my life!

# ACKNOWLEDGEMENTS

I am deeply grateful to everyone who has helped me in the preparation of this manuscript. Thank you to Caryn and Pete Cialkowski, Harold Bermont, Cheryl Southern, Debra Golden, Jennifer Fischer, and to my publisher and editor, The Floating Gallery.

I would also like to thank the following individuals for their tremendous support and encouragement: Kenneth Weine, Andrew Shepin, Constantine Shepin, Harrys Tsiartas, Andrew Pultman, Jeff Meyer, Nathaniel Bermont, Eric Bermont and Debbie Bermont.

In addition, I would like to thank The 3rd Coast Café of Chicago. Their endless cups of delicious coffee helped keep me at the top of my game while I was writing this book.

I would also like to thank my previous employers for providing me with an outstanding foundation for my success: Royal Dutch Shell Corporation, NCR Corporation, IBM Corporation and American Power Conversion Corporation.

Finally, I would like to thank each of you, the readers, for your confidence in me, in this book, and in your own ability to succeed.

# CONTENTS

## SECRET #4: CREATE A POWERFUL MESSAGE — 51

## SECRET #5: WHERE TO FIND JOB OPPORTUNITIES — 71

## SECRET #6: SELL YOURSELF — 85

## SECRET #7: PREPARE — 93

## SECRET #8: TRAITS OF IDEAL CANDIDATES — 117

# PREFACE

- **Step-by-Step Guide**
- **8 Books in 1**
- **Experience . . . Not Theory**
- **These Secrets Work**

## CONGRATULATIONS!

You have taken the first step toward obtaining the job and career you have always wanted. This book is written to give you an *unfair* advantage in your job search. After reading this book you'll feel great about yourself and the job hunt. Most importantly, *you'll interview to win!*

## A COMPLETE STEP-BY-STEP GUIDE TO JOB HUNTING SUCCESS!

This book teaches you everything you need to know to get a job—and how to *sell* yourself throughout the process. If you spend 24 solid hours following the advice in this book, you will have the foundation you need to *get the job you want!*

## EIGHT BOOKS IN ONE!

You could read eight separate books on Careers, Cover Letters, Interviewing, Job Hunting/Searching, Motivation, Negotiating, Networking and Resumes, and still not get the information you'll find in this book!

## LEARN FROM EXPERIENCE . . . NOT THEORY!

This book is based on my own proven success, as a manager, as an employee and as a job seeker. I have been in your shoes. I know what you are going through, and what it will take for you to thrive in today's job market.

I have also been in the interviewers' shoes and I'll tell you what will go through their minds when they interview you. My goal in writing this book is to make *you* victorious by sharing the secrets I have learned from over 20 years of successful job hiring, job hunting and job interviewing experiences.

## THE SECRETS IN THIS BOOK . . . WORK!

Using these secrets, I have *found jobs in tough economies, received six job offers* my senior year of college, *earned numerous job promotions*, and once *landed three offers in one week*. You, too, can achieve this kind of success if you follow the tips and techniques in this book. This book will help you triumph not only in job hunting and interviewing, but also in life!

**Sit Back and Enjoy Your Journey
Along this Bridge to a Successful Job Hunt!**

# INTRODUCTION

- **A Step-by-Step Guide to Job Hunting Success**
- **Compete in a Tough Job Market**
- **Sell Yourself**
- **Eliminate Interviewing Anxiety**
- **Get Your Dream Job**

## WELCOME!

You are about to begin the journey to job hunting success! Whether you want a position in a large corporation or a small entrepreneurial firm, after reading this book, you will jump into the job hunt like a champion and *interview to win*!

## A COMPLETE STEP-BY-STEP GUIDE TO JOB HUNTING SUCCESS

This book is written to be your complete job hunting road map. The directions are logical, easy to follow and designed to show you how to get you the job you want as quickly as possible!

In reading this book you'll:

❑ Increase Your Confidence and Self-esteem

❑ Identify Your Key Selling Points

❑ Define Your Ideal Job

❑ Create Resumes and Cover Letters That Stand Out

❑ Find Job Opportunities . . . Even When They Aren't Advertised

❑ Convince Companies to Interview You . . . Even When No Jobs Are Available

❑ Prepare For The Interview So Nobody Can Defeat You

❑ Uncover The 8 Traits of Ideal Candidates

❑ Encounter The 6 Phases of a Successful Interview

❑ Get Excited About the Job Hunt and Interview to Win

## LEARN HOW TO COMPETE IN A TOUGH JOB MARKET

In any business there is competition and job hunting will be no exception. This book will show you how to distinguish yourself so *you*, not your competition, get the job you want!

## DISCOVER HOW TO SELL YOURSELF

You'll see the many similarities between job hunting and selling. The interesting thing about job interviewing is, while you are the salesperson, you are also the product. This book will help you balance both roles to get the sale—a great job offer!

## ELIMINATE INTERVIEWING ANXIETY

You'll feel so confident in yourself and have such a good game plan, that you'll actually look forward to interviewing and enjoy the process.

## GET YOUR DREAM JOB AS QUICKLY AS POSSIBLE!

That's the goal. Lets get started.

## SECRET #1

## POSITIVE ATTITUDE (Feeling Good about Yourself!)

● **5 Strategies to Develop a Positive Mental Attitude**

The first secret to any successful job hunt is a positive mental attitude. Feeling good about yourself, and having confidence in your abilities, is essential to any successful job hunt. Optimism fosters clear thought, energy, enthusiasm and productivity. Believe that you are a *great* person and you will achieve *great* things.

Developing a positive attitude can be easy. Following, I will take you through 5 strategies that in as little as 30 seconds can help you to feel good about yourself and maintain a positive mental attitude throughout your job hunt.

---

### 5 Strategies to Develop a Positive Mental Attitude

1) **YOU ARE GREAT!**

2) **Everything Happens for a Reason**

3) **YOU CAN DO IT!**

4) **Interviewing is a Numbers Game**

5) **Surround Yourself with Positive People**

---

## 1) YOU ARE GREAT!

Wait! You're wondering whether or not you're a great person? Stop right there. Every person, in his or her own way, is *great*! You don't believe me? Well, start believing! If you don't believe you are great, who will? What? You lack confidence because you feel others are better qualified? FORGET IT!

### The Word "Qualified" is Subjective

Who decides whether or not your are qualified? Do you need the USDA to place a big, blue USDA Interview Approved stamp on your forehead? Of course not . . . being qualified is totally subjective. Relax, because I will teach you how to position yourself to become qualified. By the time you finish this book you will be able to present your qualities and characteristics so no one can defeat you.

Now, before moving on, I want you to repeat after me: "I AM GREAT!" Say it loud and with conviction. Remember *Tony the Tiger* from the Kellogg's Frosted Flakes commercials and how he used to say, *"They're Grrreeeeaaaaattttttt!"* If you really want to feel good, go to a mirror, look at yourself, smile, and like Tony the Tiger yell out . . .

*"I AM GRRREEEEAAAAATTTTTTT!"*

Doesn't that feel good?

## 2) EVERYTHING HAPPENS FOR A REASON

Right now, many of you may be experiencing difficult times. Maybe that's why you purchased this book. But, don't feel sorry for yourself or make excuses for your situation. These feelings will only sabotage your efforts.

*If you were laid off or fired*, look to the positives. This is an opportunity, not a hurdle. Be proud of who you are and what you have accomplished in your life. You are a special person. Everything happens for a reason. You may not know what that reason is today. However, in five years, you will look back on this time and be glad you went through this discovery process.

One way to look to the positive is to believe that you deserve better. Tell yourself that you lost your job so you can finally be free to find the job of your dreams. Every person I know who has lost his or her job ultimately ended up in a much better situation. You will too!

*If you are graduating or are currently employed,* be full of pride and celebrate your successes and accomplishments. Believe that you are an extraordinary person and you will get the job you want.

A positive mental attitude is not only helpful in job hunting and interviewing, but in life. Whether you are dating, investing, playing sports or doing almost anything, you will be far more successful when you are confident and happy. When you feel positive about yourself and your situation, you will enjoy all that life has to offer—including job hunting!

## 3) YOU CAN DO IT!

Keep your spirits up! A great way to feel good before the interview is to yell out with joy and confidence that you can do it. Remember John Belushi's famous words from *Animal House*, when he shouted out, "Let's do it!" Like Belushi, try going to a mirror, SMILE, and scream at the top of your lungs, "I CAN DO IT!" Then repeat out loud, "I WILL GET THE JOB I WANT!" When you yell with conviction, "I CAN DO IT!" you will start to believe in yourself.

Be positive and you will succeed. Notice how it's the positive people who seem to be the happiest and most successful. People like being around upbeat people. Being optimistic is rewarding, fun and creates enthusiasm. A positive attitude is contagious and those who catch it are forever cured!

YOU CAN DO IT!

## 4) INTERVIEWING IS A NUMBERS GAME

Hang in there. The job hunt can be frustrating, especially if you have been rejected several times. But, don't let others bring you down and strip away your confidence. The fact is that for every job you don't get, you are that much closer to getting the one that is right for you.

### Even the Best Salesperson Cannot Sell to Everyone

Successful salespeople look at each rejection as a learning experience. They see selling as a numbers game. They are thankful for rejections because each rejection gets them closer to an actual sale.

Hunting for a job is just like sales. Most likely, you will not get an offer from every company that interviews you. In fact, you may get only one out of every ten interviews. If you get rejected after an interview, say to yourself, "This job wasn't a good fit. I deserve better. Besides, I am one interview closer to getting the job I really want!"

The bottom line is not to get emotionally attached to any single interview or job prospect. Instead, try to focus on the process and what you can learn from each event. After all, not every job will be the right job for you. By remembering that interviewing is a numbers game, you will maintain the proper frame of mind to succeed.

## 5) SURROUND YOURSELF WITH POSITIVE PEOPLE

When going through an arduous job hunt, it is easy to be sidetracked by negative thoughts, but you must avoid it. Dwelling on the negative will not help. Instead, surround yourself with encouraging people. Their confidence and support will rub off on you and you will start thinking like a winner!

### Job Hunting is Similar in Concept
### to a Tenet of Real Estate

They say it is always better to buy the cheapest house in an expensive neighborhood than to buy the most expensive house in a cheap neighborhood. The value of the less expensive house in a good neighborhood is boosted by the presence of the more expensive ones. When you surround yourself with positive and motivated people, their enriching attitudes will rub off on you and boost your morale and success. If you surround yourself with positive influences, you will succeed as your value and marketability increases.

So, surround yourself with positive friends and family. If you have negative friends, stay away from them while you're job hunting. If members of your family are negative, tell them to keep their thoughts to themselves unless they have something constructive to say. I know this can be difficult, especially when dealing with family, but attitude is so important!

### Attitude Often Determines Whether
### or Not You Get the Job

So, be positive and confident, and you will succeed!

# POSITIVE ATTITUDE

## Checklist Summary

✔ Say out loud . . . "I AM GREAT!"

✔ EVERYTHING HAPPENS FOR A REASON

✔ INTERVIEWING is a NUMBERS GAME

✔ Surround yourself with POSITIVE PEOPLE

✔ Smile and shout in the mirror . . .
  "I CAN DO IT!"

*"A positive attitude is contagious
and those who catch it are forever cured!"*

# SECRET #2

## IDENTIFY YOUR KEY SELLING POINTS

- **4 Cornerstones of Personal Strengths**
- **Personal Strengths Worksheet**
- **Top 4 Strengths Quantification Worksheet**

**F**eeling good? I know you are, because you're on your way to success. This is the perfect time to go into Secret #2: Identify Your Key Selling Points. Here, you evaluate yourself and bring to mind your successes both on the job and in your personal life. Also, you determine the experience and strengths you can bring to the table. If you do not have job-related experience, I will show you how other expertise can be useful.

## WHY IS IT SO IMPORTANT TO KNOW YOUR STRENGTHS?

By identifying your strengths you can properly align yourself in the right career direction. Unfortunately, even the best sometimes forget to do this. A great example is the NBA's Michael Jordan. After winning three championships with the Chicago Bulls, he decided to retire from basketball to try baseball and golf. Since he was a tremendous athlete, Michael assumed he could succeed in any sport. As it turned out, he didn't excel nearly as much in those sports as he did in basketball. Fortunately, he realized this and returned to the NBA, where his talents were most aligned. He went on to win three more championships with the Bulls.

Everyone has unique strengths. I will show you how these strengths can be used as key selling points to get a job. But right now, start identifying your strengths so you can focus your efforts where you are most likely to get hired.

## HOW FAR CAN YOU GO?

Identifying your key strengths is like knowing how much gas you have in your car. If you have a full tank of gas, you can travel long distances. If you have just a quarter of a tank, you can only drive a short distance. When you review your strengths, be honest with yourself so you know what positions you can realistically consider. For example, if you are just graduating from college, it is unlikely that you will get a position as vice president. However, if you have been in the workforce for many years and have significant management experience, then it is feasible.

In your career, just as in driving, you can always put more gas in your tank and travel further. The key is to determine your destination and draw a road map of how to get there. Each job you work and each degree you receive are highways to success. The knowledge and experience you develop along your travels serve as fuel for your career.

## ASSESS YOUR PERSONALITY, SKILLS, STRENGTHS AND EXPERIENCES

In doing so, you will see how far you can realistically travel on your career roadmap. This inventory of your attributes will help you identify the jobs that you have the best opportunity to get.

## DON'T BE SHY

Everyone has positive attributes and experiences.

Conversely, everyone has weaknesses. Right now, concentrate on your strengths.

I have never been in an interview situation without being asked the question, "What are your strengths?" You, too, will be asked this, so you need to be prepared.

Examples of personal strengths include being honest, competitive, successful, driven, creative and loyal. I am going to ask you to take out a sheet of paper and write down your strengths. But, before I do this, let's discuss the 4 Cornerstones of Personal Strengths that will help you define your strengths and positioning.

---

### 4 Cornerstones of Personal Strengths

**1) Personality Traits**

**2) Accomplishments**

**3) Work Experience**

**4) Career Knowledge**

---

1) **Personality Traits**—This first category is broken up into two parts: General Personality Traits and Job-Related Personality Traits. *General Personality Traits* illustrates your personality. Are you an easygoing individual? Do you have an outgoing personality? Descriptions such as positive, creative, competitive, good listener, empathetic, assertive, flexible and motivated are in this category. *Job-Related Personality Traits* describe strengths of your personality that are work related. Team worker, knowledge worker, strategic thinker, natural leader, conscientious, multi-tasking, detail-oriented and problem-solver are examples of job-related strengths.

2) **Accomplishments**—This cornerstone provides insight into how versatile you are. Again, I segment accomplishments by both personal and work-related. *Personal Accomplishments* focus on your life outside of work. Examples include charitable activities, community service, offices held, etc. *Work Accomplishments* demonstrate the successes you've had in your jobs. Getting a great review, making the "100% Club", winning a company award, being featured in a corporate magazine and job promotions are all examples of work accomplishments.

3) **Work Experience**—For those of you who have it, work experience is the most important category. Those of you who don't have work experience should try to find experiences from your personal life that can demonstrate work-related skills. Work Experience describes what you have done in your career. "Managed people," "reduced expenses," "implemented local area network rollout" and "trained customer service representatives" are all examples of work experience. Try to be quantitative where applicable. If you reduced expenses, how much did you reduce them? If you managed people, how many did you manage?

4) **Career Knowledge**—Unlike work experience, career knowledge focuses on what you know—not what you have done. Those of you without work experience can put more emphasis on career knowledge. Career Knowledge is what you have learned that will help you on the job you are trying to get. If you are trying to get a computer job, knowledge such as "C++," "NT," "SNMP," and "TCP/IP" is beneficial. If you were going for an inventory management position, then knowledge such as "Just-In-Time (JIT)" and "Vertical Process Management" is appropriate.

## DECIDE WHAT MAKES YOU SO GREAT

Now it is time for you to take a sheet of paper and brainstorm about all of your positive attributes. To make this exercise easy, I have created a simple worksheet for you to use. Write down as many attributes as possible. Keep your descriptions to three words or less.

## FEEL GOOD ABOUT YOURSELF!

In doing this exercise, you will gain focus, build your confidence, better articulate your strengths, and be more realistic in identifying the kinds of jobs you can *get*. You will realize through this exercise that you truly are a spectacular person, and this will help to keep you motivated as you proceed in your job hunt. Have fun and be proud!

## PERSONAL STRENGTHS WORKSHEET

**General Personality Traits (Outgoing, Social, Empathetic, Creative, Motivated, etc.)**

1) _____

2) _____

3) _____

**Job-Related Personality Traits (Team Worker, Natural Leader, Conscientious, Multi-Tasking, etc.)**

1) _____

2) _____

3) _____

**Personal Accomplishments (Charity, Fraternity Officer, Community Service, etc.)**

1) _____

2) _____

3) _____

**Work Accomplishments (100% Club, Manager's Award, Featured in a Company Newsletter, etc.)**

1) _____

2) _____

3) _____

## PERSONAL STRENGTHS WORKSHEET (Page 2)

**Work Experience (Managed People, Reduced Expenses, Payroll Processing, etc.)**

1) _____

2) _____

3) _____


**Career Knowledge (Certifications, Programmed in C++, CPA, Used Lotus Notes, etc.)**

1) _____

2) _____

3) _____


**Other Strengths/Additional Skills**

1) _____

2) _____

3) _____

4) _____

5) _____

6) _____

7) _____

8) _____

9) _____

## QUANTIFY YOUR TOP STRENGTHS

Did you write down some of your strengths?

Good. Next, you must identify the most important strengths from your Personal Strengths Worksheet and quantify them so they become key selling points. To quantify each selling point, be specific and write down a few bullet-points as to why that strength is relevant to the position and the company. Think, "Why does that strength make me the most qualified candidate?"

For example, as a plant supervisor, if you are a great cost-cutter, be specific: "I cut the cost of manufacturing by 25 percent." A benefit to the company you are interviewing with could be, "I can apply this expertise to cut costs in your manufacturing process."

## ARE YOU ABOUT TO GRADUATE FROM SCHOOL?

If so, then a success might be how you led a group to score high on a class project. Selling points for this are your *leadership* skills and your ability to work as *a team player*. Maybe you developed a web site for a class or organization. Selling points here are your *knowledge* of web design and your ability to *manage* projects.

Or, were you in charge of a fraternity/sorority fundraiser? If so, you showed *leadership* to be able to coordinate people for a common effort. You exhibited *creativity* in the idea that raised funds; *teamwork* to achieve a goal; *success* in that you raised more money than ever before; *marketing savvy* to draw so many people; and *sales skills* to get those people to participate and donate as much as they did.

Get the idea?

## DO YOU HAVE WORK EXPERIENCE?

If so, recall accomplishments from your current and previous jobs. How about the time you turned that irate customer into a happy customer, saving a huge order? Maybe you were given a great appraisal. How about the note you got from a co-worker thanking you for helping on a project? What about the fact that you made quota three years in a row? Maybe you reduced accounts receivables by 20 percent as a result of your creative efforts. Or maybe you excelled and won a corporate award or made the 100% Club.

## EVERYONE HAS PREVIOUS EXPERIENCE
## THAT CAN HELP LAND A JOB!

Good interviewers will ask you about your experience and why it's relevant to the task at hand.

Now, go back to your Personal Strengths Worksheet and decide what are your four most relevant strengths. Write them down and quantify them.

I have provided you with a worksheet to help you with this.

## TOP 4 STRENGTHS QUANTIFICATION WORKSHEET

**Strength #1:** _____

    **Benefits to Company:** _____

    _____

    _____

**Strength #2:** _____

    **Benefits to Company:** _____

    _____

    _____

**Strength #3:** _____

    **Benefits to Company:** _____

    _____

    _____

**Strength #4:** _____

    **Benefits to Company:** _____

    _____

    _____

# IDENTIFY YOUR KEY SELLING POINTS

## CHECKLIST SUMMARY

✔ Knowing your STRENGTHS focuses your JOB HUNT

✔ STRENGTHS are a combination of PERSONAL
   TRAITS, ACCOMPLISHMENTS, EXPERIENCES
   and KNOWLEDGE

✔ Complete the *PERSONAL STRENGTHS* WORKSHEET

✔ QUANTIFY your STRENGTHS

✔ Complete the *TOP 4 STRENGTHS* WORKSHEET

*"Don't be shy. Everyone has positive
attributes and experiences to offer an employer!"*

# SECRET #3

## Define the Job You Want

- **10 Ways to Define the Job You Want**
- **Job Definition Worksheet**

**N**ow you know your strengths and the jobs you *can* get. But, what type of career do you *want*? There is a big difference between what you *can* get versus what you *want* to do for a living. Defining the Job You Want is the next critical secret to job hunting.

Imagine going on a vacation and not knowing where to go or how to get there. Sounds crazy, doesn't it? Yet many people do just that when they start their job hunt. Few job seekers ask the question "What is my ideal job?" In fact, most people don't believe there is an ideal job for them. Consequently, they don't devote the time necessary to define their ultimate job. As a result, they end up being unhappy in their professions. After all, if you don't know what you want, how are you going to get it?

## WHAT ARE THE CAUSES OF JOB DISSATISFACTION?

Most people are not satisfied in their current occupations because they accepted jobs that don't align with their personal interests, skills and values. Just to earn a buck, they took a position that they *could* do, rather than one that they *wanted* to do. Hence, most people lack the motivation, creativity and desire to do their jobs well. As a result, they wind up unhappy.

## DEVELOP AN ACHIEVABLE PLAN!

Set goals that are specific, measurable and achievable. To get the job you want, you have to be particular about the type of occupation you desire. You also must be pragmatic about your abilities, drive and expertise.

## HAVE YOU EVER TAKEN THE TIME TO OUTLINE YOUR IDEAL JOB?

If not, you should! Take time to figure out what you want to do for a living.

## DO YOU WANT TO LIVE TO WORK OR WORK TO LIVE?

Have you known people who constantly complain about their job, but do nothing to change the situation? Isn't it painful to be around them?

Including commuting time (upwards to one hour each way) and actual work (usually eight hours a day), most people spend at least 50 hours a week working. Since the average person sleeps around 56 hours a week, they consume 106 hours a week between working and sleeping. There are only 168 hours in a week. That leaves only 62 hours a week of *free* time. That means you spend almost *half* of your waking hours working and commuting. Why be miserable for almost half of your life?

If you are not happy in your job, you are wasting away almost half of your life. If you don't enjoy your occupation, the stress, frustration and lack of fulfillment is going to negatively impact other facets of your life. This is why it is so important to have a job that you enjoy versus a job that just pays the bills.

The most important aspects of my life are health, love, family, friends and spirituality—and then my job. But, if my job is not enjoyable, that negatively impacts everything else. That is why throughout my career I've chosen professions where I've looked forward to work as much as leisure.

You, too, can actually enjoy work and have fun! That's right . . . FUN! The key to enjoying your occupation is to determine the qualities and characteristics of your ideal job. What do you visualize yourself doing every day and enjoying? Once you find a position that closely matches your desires, you will actually look forward to going to work each day. This enjoyment will spill over positively into other aspects of your life.

## HOW I DEFINE MY DREAM JOB

To define my ideal position, I use spreadsheets to score and rank important criteria. This helps me determine, even before the interview, the kind of job I want to have.

## Below are Sample Job Characteristics I Value the Most:

❏ FUN *(Most Important)*

❏ Freedom to work as if I was my own boss

❏ Challenging

❏ International travel

❏ Competitive

❏ The company is a leader in its industry

❏ The people I work with are smart, driven and motivated

❏ Financially rewarding

❏ If I succeed, I will be recognized and promoted

❏ The job matches my values and beliefs

These are just some of the job characteristics that are important to me. What are the qualities that are important to you? Are you unsure? If so, let's look at 10 Ways to Define the Job You Want. Throughout this process, consider your strengths and key selling points. Ask yourself if there is a match between your strengths and your ideal job characteristics.

### 10 Ways to Define the Job You Want

1) **Type of Job**

2) **Type of Industry**

3) **Type of Company**

4) **Career Path**

5) **Job Structure**

6) **Work Hours**

7) **Travel**

8) **Office Setting**

9) **Location**

10) **Compensation and Benefits**

## 1) TYPE OF JOB

The first step you must take is to determine the *type* of job that really interests you.

This may appear trivial, but you would be amazed at how many people have no idea what really interests them.

What kinds of jobs allow you to utilize your strengths? Which of these jobs can you see yourself going to each day? Does accounting interest you? If not, how about architecture or public relations? Could truck driving be your dream job? Maybe software development is best?

Job satisfaction is in the eye of the beholder. For example, if your passion in life is cleaning and organizing, then a job as a housekeeper may appeal to you. Driving a truck could be tempting to someone who likes to travel, see the country and meet new people. Software developing can be ideal for someone who loves the challenge of taking a concept and turning it into a successful product.

### Only You Can Decide Where Your Passion Rests!

Don't listen to what others say you should be. Had I listened to others, I would have gone to medical school to become a doctor. But, I get woozy at the sight of blood and medical instruments. I don't think I would have lasted too long in medical school. Medicine is not my passion.

### Decide What Interests You!

There are millions of ways to earn a buck. People who like their jobs tend to live longer and happier lives than those who detest going to work each day. Job stress causes people to lose sleep and lead unhealthy lifestyles. When I am under pressure or frustrated, often that unhappiness manifests itself into illness. My worst maladies have always coincided with times I was most stressed about my job.

People who constantly complain about their jobs do not feel they control their own destiny. Many will stay in jobs they dislike their entire lives because they feel that every job will lead to dissatisfaction. But that's just not true. If you choose to do something you can have fun with, you can actually enjoy going to work each day.

I enjoy working even more than vacation because I love helping people and interacting with others. I also thrive on competition and the thrill of the ride. I have worked in situations I hated, and that's why I quit those jobs. Life is too short to do something you don't enjoy. So, clear your mind and think about the following questions.

"What jobs allow me to best capitalize on my strengths and unique selling points?"

"If I could do any occupation in the world, what would I choose?"

## 2) TYPE OF INDUSTRY

Once you have decided on the type of job that interests you, your next goal is to determine your *ideal* industry. When I graduated from college, I received six job offers. I knew I wanted to be a salesperson, but what did I want to sell? The two offers that interested me most were NCR (a computer manufacturer) and U.S. Steel (a leader in the steel industry). U.S. Steel offered me a starting salary of 25 percent more than NCR. Basically, the choice for me boiled down to—"Do I want to be in the steel industry or the computer industry?"

I chose the computer industry and accepted the offer from NCR even though it was for less money. I never regretted that decision. Both were, and still are, tremendous companies. I just opted for the industry that interested me the most. Prior to starting my coaching, speaking and publishing business, I spent fourteen years in the computer industry—and loved it! I thrived on the constant change, abundant opportunities and rapid innovations.

### Just One Decision Can Effect
### the Entire Course of Your Life!

Choosing an industry is not a decision to be made lightly. Had I chosen the steel industry, my whole life would have been different—not just my career, but my experiences and friends. I would have lived in a different city, because the offer that I accepted was in St. Louis and the one I rejected was in Detroit.

Perhaps more importantly, once a person chooses an industry, depending on that industry and career, a person typically stays for a minimum of three different jobs within that industry. Rarely do people switch industries because of the experience and knowledge they gain through each job. Once that expertise is acquired, it is very difficult to discard that investment, switch industries, and risk being unable to apply that knowledge to a new area.

Sound scary? It's true. So take some time and make sure you know what really interests you. Ask yourself, "With my strengths, experiences and key selling points, which industries should consider?"

## 3) TYPE OF COMPANY

Next, ask yourself what type of company you want to join. Do you want to work for a company that is publicly traded or private? Do you seek a company that promotes from within or one that hires from the outside? What kind of management philosophies do you value? Do you want the prestige of a big established company or do you want the challenge and opportunity that a smaller start-up offers?

There is prestige and opportunity for training and growth that comes with working for a company with a *household* name. However, big companies often have a lot of politics, bureaucracies and rules. What is more important to you? These are important issues to consider when deciding the type of company that is right for you.

## 4) CAREER PATH

Now that you have decided your ideal job, industry and type of company, your next decision is to determine which career path to take. This will be your road map (plan).

What is your ultimate destination? Some people want to be an engineer their entire career. Others want to become a manager. Some want to shoot for the top and become the leader of a company. What do you want?

If you think you want to go into management, do you have the strengths and expertise to do so *now*? If not, are you capable of learning what you need to know to succeed? If the answer is yes, make sure you interview with companies that are growing and promote from within. Then, identify the types of jobs that will give you the experience you'll need to become a manager in that company.

If you want to be in sales your entire career, research industries and companies with the highest salaries, the best perks and the most promising futures for their top salespeople. For instance, in the 1980s everyone wanted to get into real estate. In the 1990s, Enterprise and Year 2000 software sales positions were most in demand. But what happened to Year 2000 software salespeople after the year 2000? Who knows? Make sure you choose a career path leading to a good future. No one wants a dead-end job.

## 5) JOB STRUCTURE

Although you know the type of job that you want, similar jobs can have totally different structures. For instance, if you look at sales, you can have a job that is a part of a team or one where you are on your own. You can have compensation based on Management by Objective (MBO) or compensation based strictly on sales revenue or sales growth.

What kind of job structure is ideal for you?

Do you want a job with set goals and objectives?

Do you want a job where you are told exactly what to do—or one where you help in determining ongoing strategic decisions?

Maybe you want a job where you are part of a team and are compensated according to the team's successes. Conversely, you might prefer a situation where you work independently and recognized solely for your own efforts. Do you want to work on short-term or long-term projects?

You've heard the expression "You can't place a square peg in a round hole." If you take a job that doesn't match the structure you are looking for, you will feel like a "square peg." Typically, "square pegs" end up complaining about their jobs and seem to always be miserable. You don't want that, do you? That's why it is so important to identify the kind of structure that is best suited to you (i.e. your personality, work ethics, and skills).

## 6) WORK HOURS

Have you ever thought about how long and how hard you want to work? Do you mind working 50 to 60 hours a week? Or would you rather work only 40 hours? Do you want to work part-time or full-time? Many jobs today require far more than the traditional 9-to-5 schedule. Often you could be required to work long hours, late at night, and sometimes on weekends. Is this a sacrifice you are willing to make? Examples of professions that require extensive hours are consulting, retail, real estate, computer programming, legal, health care and hotel management.

It is up to you. If you value balance in your life, then work hours are important. If you are one who wants to succeed and climb the career ladder at all costs, then work hours may not be a big deal to you. Either way, you need to decide up front.

## 7) TRAVEL

Travel is another factor to consider when looking for a job. Some jobs require extensive travel, where others demand little to no travel. If you enjoy traveling, then a desk job may not appeal to you. However, if you have a family you don't want to be away from, it may be best to have a job where you go to the same location every day.

## 8) OFFICE SETTING

Many people enjoy working because of the mental stimulation they get from being around other motivated people. If you like being around others, then a large office environment may be optimal. Some like the freedom of working on their own without the need for direct supervision. In this case, working out of the home may be more appealing. When looking at potential jobs, consider the following questions.

### Do You Want to Work at a Corporate
### Headquarters or a Remote Location?

A remote location is good if you want to remain somewhat anonymous or independent. However, if you want to get promoted and be on the fast track, you may want to be at headquarters where you are visible to key corporate managers and your contributions can be seen first hand.

### Do You Want to Work in an Office
### Building Or Out of Your Home?

An office provides camaraderie and close proximity to your boss. However, working out of the home provides more autonomy. Since you don't have to commute, working out of the home allows you to have more time to yourself. But, you lose access to meeting as many new people as being in an office environment. Balance what aspects are most important to you.

### Are You Comfortable Working in a Cubicle
### or Do You Need an Office?

Some people, like me, enjoy working with background noise; others need the silence of an office.

### Do You Want to Wear Business Casual
### or Professional Clothing?

While I like wearing casual clothing, other people enjoy dressing more formally. Which style is more comfortable for you?

## 9) LOCATION

In today's global economy, you could end up receiving job offers from all over the world. Have you ever thought about where you wanted to live? Often people have chosen to move to another city strictly because of a job. Before you do that, you need to be honest with yourself about what is important in your life.

I used to think my career was the most important aspect of my life.

That was until I relocated to Raleigh, North Carolina, for a job promotion. At the time of my move, Raleigh was named the top region (to live) in the country. Thousands of people were flocking there. I took the promotion without having ever seen Raleigh. I was filled with excitement and within three weeks, I was on my way to North Carolina.

At the time of my move, I was single and knew no one in Raleigh.

The first year, the job went fantastically well. I was earning more than ever before, had success and recognition within the company, and traveled to exciting places. But, during the beginning of the second year in Raleigh, I started to question my decision. Even though I was earning a great income, I was not happy. I started to feel a real void in my life.

### Have You Ever Been Unhappy and Couldn't Figure Out Why?

At first, I couldn't figure out what it was. One day, I finally realized that I missed my family and friends. I didn't recognize how important a local support structure was to me until I no longer had it. Until then, I didn't understand the importance of balance in my life. I finally understood that work and money were not the sole sources of happiness. I finally understood that health, love, family, friends and spirituality were far more important to me than the job.

Now, I am happily back in Chicago. I am especially glad I moved back because, as it turned out, my mother became very sick and ultimately passed away within two years of my return. Had I stayed in Raleigh, I would have missed out on the time I spent with my dear mother during those final two years of her life. If you are close to your family, you may want to work in the same metropolitan area as them. If not, at least the Internet and phone provide ways to stay in touch.

### How Important is Balance to You?

Only you know where you want to live and how important it is to be near your family and friends. Every city has its pluses and minuses. I recommend that before you pick up and move for a job, ask yourself if you can still keep balance in your life. Then ask yourself if you can still live within the values of what is important to you. You will be glad you did.

Wow! I'll bet you didn't realize how many dynamics you should consider when thinking about your ideal job. In all honesty, they are the *key factors* in determining whether you have the job of your dreams or an unhappy career move.

## 10) COMPENSATION & BENEFITS

Finally, the tenth aspect to consider is compensation and benefits. You might love your job, but if you are not making enough money to live the kind of lifestyle you want to live, you won't be happy. If compensation and benefits are important to you, there are several areas of compensation to explore.

a) **Base Salary or Hourly Wage Desired?** How much do you want to make? How much do you realistically need to earn to live the lifestyle you want? Do you want a salary or an hourly position?

b) **Bonus vs. Commission?** If you choose a profession that has leveraged compensation, do you want quarterly bonuses or annual? Are you looking for salary plus commission or do you want a higher commission rate where the compensation may be commission versus a draw on salary?

c) **Profit Sharing?** Do you want to work for a company that shares its profits with its employees or a company that may have better benefits?

d) **Housing Allowance?** Do you want to work out of your home? If so, do you have room in your house to work? How much of a housing allowance do you need to make it worthwhile?

e) **Car Allowance vs. Company Car?** Does the occupation you want require you to drive frequently? If so, are you willing to let the company dictate the kind of car you can drive? Do you want a car allowance so you can choose the car, or would you be okay with a company car the boss picks out, but includes insurance?

f) **Stock Options?** Many companies offer stock options in lieu of higher salaries. Are you willing to sacrifice salary for stock options? Is the stock likely to increase? What is an optimal vesting period? How long do you have to hold the stock before you can sell?

g) **Retirement Plans?** Do you prefer a company with a 401(k) program or Employee Stock Ownership Plan (ESOP)? If there is a 401(k), what is the desired company match? Do you want to have access to mutual funds in your 401(k)? What vesting timeframe is acceptable to you? Maybe, you want to work a government job where there is a pension plan. If so, you need to consider the plan's funding, security and contribution requirements.

h) **Medical Benefits?** Do you have a favorite doctor or are you willing to use an HMO? How about dental and eye care, are they important to you? If so, are you willing to accept an HMO, or pay a higher deductible to get the expanded coverage? Will you accept higher deductibles in exchange for lower co-pays? Would you require disability and life insurance?

i) **Raise Policies?** Will you tolerate a company that limits pay raises to 10 percent in exchange for more job security? Are you willing to work for a company where you have to "walk on water" to get a raise, but you get great perks? What is your expectation of a fair raise policy?

**j)** **Perks?** Corporate day care, expense accounts, golf club memberships, on-site exercise clubs, discounts at local merchants, and education reimbursements are all potential perks. What are the important perks for you? Are you willing to sacrifice some perks for more pay?

## Compensation Is One of the Biggest Culprits of Employee Dissatisfaction

You should spend some serious time developing a budget and figuring out what you need to earn in order to be happy with your job. While compensation is not the sole determinant of job satisfaction, it can hold significant weight. Many people have not thought through what they are worth and what they expect to earn. This is a big mistake. If you decide in advance what you are looking for, you will be much more focused and successful in finding a job that excites you. Look at all aspects of compensation.

Some companies make up for lower salary and bonus earnings by providing phenomenal benefits and perks. One large brewer used to give its employees a free case of beer every month. One large beverage company gives its employees unlimited free cola. Some companies have their own day care and exercise facilities. These perks can save hundreds, if not thousands of dollars every month. Everything doesn't just boil down to W-2 earnings.

Once you know what you want, you will be much more focused, efficient and successful in your job hunt. Also, you will convey the image of a goal-oriented person. That will come across loud and clear in an interview, and will set you above your competition.

## Now, Define Your Ideal Job

While what you just read is fresh in your mind, list at least ten characteristics you want in your ideal job. If you prefer guidance, I have provided you with a worksheet. Once you have identified your ideal job, try to summarize your ideal job description or goal into a one-to-two sentence personal mission statement. Post this mission statement on your wall and in your notebooks and journals. If you constantly focus on your goal, and not the process, you will achieve what you want and subsequently enjoy the process.

## IDEAL JOB DEFINITION WORKSHEET

**Type of Job(s):**      1)_____

2)_____

3)_____

**Type of Industry(s):**   1)_____

2)_____

3)_____

**Type of Company:**   Privately Held: _____ Publicly Held: _____

Fortune 500 Company: _____

Small/Midsize Company:_____

Conservative: _____ Liberal: _____

High Growth: _____ Turnaround Possibility: _____

**Desired Career Path:**

Year 1) _____

Year 2) _____

Year 3) _____

Year 4) _____

Year 5) _____

**Ideal Job Structure:**  _____

_____

**Desired Hours Worked:**      **Per Day:** _____      **Per Week:** _____

## IDEAL JOB DEFINITION WORKSHEET (Page 2)

**Travel:** Yes \_\_\_\_ No \_\_\_\_ **If Yes, How Much Travel:** _____

**Work out of Home or Office?** _____

**Type of Office Environment Desired:** _____

**Casual or Formal Work Environment?** _____

**City(s) You Can Work In:** _____

**Compensation Benefits:** _____

_____

**What Motivates You?** _____

_____

**Top 4 Personal Strengths:** _____

_____

_____

_____

**Ideal Job Mission Statement:** _____

_____

# DEFINE THE JOB YOU WANT

## CHECKLIST SUMMARY

✔ Job DISSATISFACTION is caused by a MISMATCH between your VALUES and your JOB

✔ Don't LIVE to work . . . WORK TO LIVE!

✔ Almost HALF of your LIFE is spent on work . . . ENJOY IT!

✔ Only YOU can decide your PASSION

✔ Complete the *IDEAL JOB DEFINITION* WORKSHEET

✔ Determine how important BALANCE is in your LIFE

*"If you don't know what you want, how are you going to get it?"*

## CREATE A POWERFUL MESSAGE
- **10 Keys to Writing Powerful Resumes**
- **4 Cs of Awesome Cover Letters**

**H**ave you completed the exercise on defining your ideal job? If not, MAKE YOUR LIST NOW! Then, compare your ideal job list with your Personal Strengths Worksheet and resolve any differences between the two that could cause you to lose your focus.

By now you know the kinds of companies and occupations that interest you. So, how are you going to get an interview at one of these companies? Well, how do companies like Nike and Budweiser get you to buy their products?

## ADVERTISING

In fact, these two industry giants are masters of advertising. Advertising is the vehicle that communicates the message about the product. Advertising is what generates interest.

What does advertising have to do with interviewing? Well, remember *you* are the product being sold. To build *your* brand awareness, you must have a powerful message to advertise. The way that you position yourself, and create a powerful message about you, is through your resumes and cover letters. Just as an advertisement needs to be good to sell its product, so do resumes and cover letters. In fact, your resumes and cover letters must be outstanding!

## WHY ARE CERTAIN PRODUCTS POPULAR?

How did products like Evian, Tropicana and BMW become so popular with consumers?

Because they are great products that have fantastic marketing and advertising. We already know that *you* are a great product, so let's focus on how to advertise your skills.

Like most ads, the more copy (words) you have in your cover letters and resumes, the less people will remember them. Some of the most popular ads have been those that are simple. Think of Nike's "Just Do IT!" campaign—simple but powerful. The original Nike ads did a great job of creating excitement through candid and forceful simplicity.

Thus, for you to excel in the job hunt, you need to create a powerful message. Your resumes and cover letters should be short and powerful advertisements that every company will remember. Just as you see hundreds of advertisements a day, human resource departments receive hundreds of resumes and cover letters. Your resumes and cover letters have to stand out to be noticed.

## YOU DON'T HAVE TO SAY TOO MUCH IN YOUR RESUMES AND COVER LETTERS

Just say enough to create interest. The sole purpose of the resume and cover letter is to get you the interview. A *powerful* resume and cover letter will not land you a job, but a *weak* combination will cost you one!

To create a powerful message—one that will secure you an interview—you need to tailor your resumes and cover letters. Adapt them to the position and the company you are seeking. Use your resumes and cover letters as advertisements of your success. Include information and vocabulary in your message that is appropriate for your target audience.

## EACH OCCUPATION AND INDUSTRY REQUIRES A MESSAGE WITH UNIQUE WORDING

If you want a job in information technology, use words such as "SNMP," "Java," and "Relational Database" in your message. If you are seeking an accounting position, you would use words such as "ledger," "financial statement," "receivables," and "inventories."

## THE MESSAGE SHOULD BE SHORT AND SWEET

Many people make the mistake of having multiple page resumes and cover letters that are full of useless information. Typically, multiple-page resumes and cover letters are littered with opinions, lacking in facts, and are flat-out BORING! I have read many that literally put me to sleep. In fact, if a message is opinionated and lacks facts and excitement, I will reject that person immediately and toss the resume and cover letter in the circular file. Do you think I'm being harsh? Well, this is reality.

## POWERFUL RESUMES HAVE TEN ATTRIBUTES IN COMMON

Thus far, I have covered some basics in creating a powerful message in both resumes and cover letters. In the pages to follow I will discuss each vehicle in more detail. First, let's focus on the resume. For any resume to be successful, it must have ten specific attributes.

---

### 10 Keys to Writing Powerful Resumes

1) Concise

2) Factual

3) Action-Oriented

4) Easy-to-Read

5) One-to-Two Pages

6) Position-Relevant

7) Sensible

8) Critiqued

9) Internet-Ready

10) Attractive/Creative

---

## 1) CONCISE

In as few words as possible, make your points short and concise.

The fewer words the better.

## 2) FACTUAL

Nothing will turn off interviewers more than a resume filled with opinions and essays. Keep to the facts. If, you were tremendously successful in eliminating wasteful spending in your previous job, then state something like, "Reduced expenses by 35 percent." That comes across as powerful and factual, advertising loud and clear that you are a great cost cutter.

If you are in sales, I am sure you will want to tell interviewers that you are the world's greatest salesperson and that you can sell ice to an Eskimo or sand in the desert. Give them some great impressions like, "Achieved 100% Club five years in a row," "Grew sales 65 percent year after year," and "Won five corporate management awards." Now those are some powerful and factual statements. Wouldn't you be impressed?

The main message here is to state facts that will be important and relevant to interviewers. These will stick out in their minds and they will remember your resume, both during and after your interview.

## 3) ACTION-ORIENTED

The best resumes contain action words. Action words bring your experience to life and get you noticed. Examples of action words that can create interest in your resume include:

| | | | | |
|---|---|---|---|---|
| Negotiated | Grew | Managed | Reduced | Increased |
| Programmed | Directed | Implemented | Achieved | Coordinated |
| Developed | Streamlined | Wrote | Trained | Generated |
| Established | Initiated | Eliminated | Evaluated | Strengthened |
| Utilized | Organized | Supervised | Led | Created |
| Participated | Improved | Presented | Demonstrated | Collaborated |

## 4) EASY-TO-READ

Many people cram so many words on their resume that the reader has no clue where to start. You want your resume to be "easy on the eyes." The reader should be able to find relevant information quickly. On average, interviewers will take about fifteen seconds to scan your credentials (resume). If, in fifteen seconds, they cannot find what they are looking for, most likely your resume will be wadded up and tossed with a bank shot off the cubicle wall, and with any luck, into the wastepaper basket. (*Interviewers get so much practice . . . they just hate it when they miss the basket.*) Interviewers look for what you will bring to the job and company. Make it easy for them to see why they should interview you!

### There Are 2 Types of Resumes

There are two methods of creating an easy-to-read resume. The first way to organize your resume is *chronological*. A chronological resume is structured by the date(s) you were employed, from your most recent job to your least.

A chronological resume is constructed by listing by date your job history and accomplishments. On the left column of the resume, you place titles such as "Profile," "Expertise," and "Education." In the right column of the resume, fill in the details. Important facts to include are job description, job accomplishments and time frames of employment.

The second way you can organize your resume is *functional*. Here, you list your accomplishments by job description or job function instead of by date. The functional resume may be more useful if you have lapses in time where you were unemployed or chose not to work. Since large lapses in time can be a red flag to a reader, you may be better suited with the functional approach.

However, if you have a good work history, I recommend the chronological approach over the functional approach. As a person who has read thousands of resumes, I feel it is easier to learn about a person's career progression with the chronological approach.

## 5) A MAXIMUM OF TWO PAGES IN LENGTH

I am a big advocate of a resume being contained to a maximum of two pages in length. Why? Because, I can't scan a resume longer than two pages in fifteen seconds and neither can anyone else. (The only value of a multiple-page resume is that it weighs more when wadded up, thus providing a better chance of making the basket into the garbage can on the first try.)

The resume is an advertisement that creates interest in you. Your resume should create just enough curiosity for the reader to want to interview you. This can easily be accomplished in one or two pages.

The key here is to place the most recent and relevant information on the resume. Quite honestly, it doesn't matter what you did fifteen or twenty years ago. Most likely, you have forgotten much of that knowledge anyway. What is important to interviewers is, "What have you done lately?" This can be expressed succinctly in one or two pages.

## 6) POSITION-RELEVANT

Many resumes are muddied with personal items that have no relevance to the reader.

As a result, people often put themselves at a disadvantage before they get the chance to interview. If something personal needs to be said, say it in the interview. People have been known to put interests, hobbies, political beliefs, and even religious beliefs on the resume. This is unwise. Why give interviewers information that could get you rejected even before the interview? Interviewers like to hire people with interests and basic values similar to their own.

When you keep the information on your resume strictly business, you will have more room on your resume for what is really important—*Position-Relevant Information.*

Position-Relevant Information (PRI) is the information that has a significant impact in the decision-making process for job selection. The best way to test each statement in your resume for PRI is to ask the question, "So what?" Put yourself in the interviewer's shoes. Look at the position. Then ask yourself the question, "So what?"

Let's say you want to include in your resume the statement, "Proficient at Microsoft Word and Lotus 123." So what? Well, if you are interviewing for a secretarial position, this could be useful. However, if you are interviewing for a sales position selling surgical instruments, it may be less than relevant.

PRI is what interviewers care about. It can be challenging to know what PRI to include when every company and potential position is unique. But it is important to tailor your resume whenever possible.

### Put Yourself in the Shoes of the Interviewer

You can determine the appropriate PRI by putting yourself in the position of your potential boss. Imagine you were the person doing the interview. What would be important? If the position is for product management, then an MBA, prior experience and ability to communicate, may be the PRI. What if you are interviewing for an engineering position or a project manager position? Then the PRI might be project history, significant outcomes or accomplishments, and time of project completion.

When putting statements into your resume, ask yourself, "Is it PRI?" Does the information pass the "So what?" test? If so, use it. If not, leave it out.

## 7) SENSIBLE

Don't tell more than you need to when creating a powerful resume. A great resume should contain only sensible information. Quite often, I have seen resumes where people place desired salary on the resume. This is a bad idea because you will put yourself at a great disadvantage.

First, if your compensation is too high, you will be rejected without even having the chance to sell the company on why you are worth it. If your compensation is too low, the company will not think you have the skills or confidence necessary for the job, and reject you. And if you are in the ballpark, then you have placed a cap on what your job offer can be, because no company will offer you more than a 15 percent to 20 percent increase over what you are making now. Why limit your potential? There is absolutely *no* need to put compensation history in your resume!

### Do Not List Weaknesses on Your Resume

Weaknesses include jobs where you unintentionally lasted only a short time (less than three months) and any other information that could negatively reflect on you as a person. Keep the resume focused on business.

Most important, don't give away all of your best information—you want to save some great zingers for the interview! The resume is the advertisement that gets you the interview. Just as most people don't buy a product solely because of an ad, you will not get the job solely because of your resume. However, if you have a powerful resume, you will have many more interviews.

## 8) CRITIQUED

The most important thing you can do before you finish is to proofread the resume. Use your word processor's spelling and grammar check. Then, have others critique it. Sometimes you can get too close to your creation and miss obvious mistakes that your software does not catch. I know in writing this book my spelling and grammar check missed several mistakes that only others could detect. The more people who critique your resume, the better!

I am always amused and amazed at how many people have mistakes in their resumes.

### Some Examples of Crazy Mistakes are Listed Below:

"Reason for leaving last job: maturity leave."

"I have lurnt the Word Perfect 6.0 computor progrom."

"Received a plague for Salesperson of the Month."

"I require a salary commiserate with my extensive expertise."

### Please Stick to Position-Relevant Information!

In addition, proof the resume to make sure what you are saying meets the PRI. You wouldn't believe some of the crazy things people have put in resumes.

### Here are some more examples
### of unbelievable quotes:

"Note: Please, don't misconstrue my 10 jobs as 'job hopping,' I have never quit a job."

"Let's get together, so you can 'ooh' and 'aah' over my experience."

"You will want me to be Head Honcho in no time."

"It's best for employers that I not work with people."

"I was working for my dad until he decided to move."

"Marital status: Single, unmarried, unengaged, uninvolved. No commitments."

"I have an fantastic track record, although I am not a racehorse."

"I am loyal to my employer . . . feel free to respond to my resume on my office e-mail."

"I have become completely paranoid, trusting no one and absolutely nothing."

"I procrastinate, especially when the task is unpleasant."

"Personal interests: Donating blood. Fifteen gallons so far."

"References: None. I've left a path of destruction."

"Am a perfectionist and rarely if ever forget the Details."

"Marital status: Often. Children: Various."

"Reason for leaving last job: They insisted that all employees get to work by 9:00 am."

"My boss made me a scapegoat, just like my three previous employers."

## 9) INTERNET-READY

More and more companies are asking for resumes to be sent via e-mail.

Once the company receives your resume via e-mail, the resume is scanned for key words. To maximize efficiency, many firms use a computer to read resumes first. Computers decipher which resumes should be reviewed by using pre-selected criteria based on a defined subset of key words and phrases.

So, how can you create a technology-friendly resume? First, you can create a version of your resume where you eliminate all major formatting. Formats such as underlining, tabs, bolding, and italicizing all give e-mail gateways a major headache. When you format using any of those, the resume arrives at the company unreadable.

While an Internet-ready resume is not attractive, you need to create a basic resume where all you have are carriage returns, blank lines, and space bar blanks that replace tabs. Also, many e-mail systems can't handle more than seventy-nine characters on a line. So be judicious in what you say, and reduce the formatting to a minimum and you will have a winning online resume.

### Use "Buzz Words"

Since computers often scan resumes before humans do, it is important to use industry "buzz words" or key words on your resume. Examples of key words for computer industry professions are "Java," "C++," "ATM," etc. Examples of "buzz words" for legal professions are "litigated," "class action," "awarded," "negligence," etc. Determine the most common phrases for the industry that interests you and include them where appropriate. Action words, as mentioned earlier, are also critical, because computers will look for those as well.

### Online Resumes

You can go to one of many Internet sites and create a resume online. There are many free and fee based sites where you complete an online form that stores your resume in a database with thousands of others, so potential employers can scan them. Technology is improving this process every day. Often you can cut and paste parts of your Internet-ready resume right into their online forms.

You can also consider converting your resume into Adobe Acrobat format. Most everyone who uses the Internet has Acrobat on their computer and will be able to read your resume with this software.

To summarize, not only should you have a printed version of your resume, you should also have your resume in one or two formats that can be used for online distribution.

## 10) ATTRACTIVE/CREATIVE

Your resume, like an advertisement, must look good. Have others read your resume and give you pointers. Look at your resume a day or two later to get a fresh perspective of it. Make sure that it is attractive and communicates effectively.

For printed resumes, use only high quality (heavier bond) paper—not copier paper. There is something to be said for paper with a substantial feel—it conveys a good image. Use fonts, colors, layouts and words that create uniqueness without compromising its professionalism.

For both printed and online resumes, to be powerful, they also need to be creative. In addition to the action words described earlier, use words that express strength and confidence. For example, the phrase "proficient at" is far stronger than "learned." Proficient means that not only did you learn something, you know it inside and out. An attractive and creative resume will be the honey that attracts interviewers and lands you job opportunities.

## References Available upon Request

Before leaving the topic of resumes I want to cover one final point—*references*. There is no need to list references on your resume. Different interviewers will want to speak with different kinds of references. Others may not need references at all. So on the bottom of your resume, you can either just say "References Available upon Request" or not put anything at all.

With that being said, it is still a good idea to put together a list of references in case you get a request. Just keep the list separate, not on the resume. Try to get a combination of work and personal references. Two of each is sufficient. Make sure you have accurate information for each reference including name, address, phone #, position, employer, e-mail, and length of time you have known the reference. It is common practice only to list references that you have known for at least one year. Call each reference before you use them to get their okay to be utilized, and to make sure they will be a good reference. Many a good job opportunity has been lost because a person did not contact their references before using them.

## Resume Summary

You need a great resume to open the door to most interview opportunities. At this point, you should know the basics of writing a successful resume. Following, I will give you examples of a resume in both chronological and functional formats (print versions). I will also provide you a sample chronological resume in an online format. However, if you are still not comfortable writing your ideal resume, do not despair. There are many "how to" books dedicated to writing resumes. You can find these books in the same section of the library or bookstore where you found this book. Also, there are entire books that discuss how to write resumes for online distribution.

While walking through a computer super store recently, I noticed several computer programs on how to write resumes. Also many word processing packages have resume templates built in. The advantage of creating a resume on your computer is that you can *tailor* each resume to a particular job and company. If you do create a resume on your computer, make sure you have a high quality laser printer or "laser quality" ink-jet printer. Make certain that you convey a professional image. If you do not have a high quality printer, create the resume, save it to a diskette, and go to a local copy shop and print your resume there.

**Now, go create a POWERFUL resume!**

# SAMPLE CHRONOLOGICAL RESUME

## Todd L. Bermont

**PROFILE**

Self-employed author, motivational speaker, and sales trainer with over 15 years of executive management and corporate sales experience.

**EXPERTISE**

\* Sales Management \* OEM and F1000 Key Account Management
\* Sales Training \* Compensation Plan Design \* Increasing Attach Rates
\* Territory Management \* New Business Development \* Interviewing
\* Global Business Development \* People Development \* Hiring
\* Project Management \* Product Development \* Customer Satisfaction
\* Cross Selling \* Market Share and Competitive Analysis \* Negotiation

**EXPERIENCE**

**<u>10 Step Corporation</u>**

**President (Feb, '00 – Present)**

10 Step Corporation specializes in helping companies and individuals succeed through coaching, training, and motivational speaking. Responsibilities include presiding over sales, marketing, accounting, logistics, inventory, investments, publishing, consulting, speaking, and human resources.

**<u>Red XYZ Corporation</u>**

**Director, Strategic Partnership Organization (November, '95 – January, '00)**

Managed global partnerships with leading computer vendors.

Supervised direct reports in US & coordinated additional indirect people in Europe & Asia Partnerships included a mix of "Buy-Sell" and "Meet-in-the Channel" relationships.

Grew year-over-year sales more than triple the growth rate of Red XYZ.

Additional achievements included increasing attach rates, profitability, customer satisfaction, and market share.

**Channel Manager, Fortune Accounts (June, '94 – September, '95)**

Managed the Fortune 1000 Channel. Key accomplishments included growing average territory sales over 300 percent, while simultaneously increasing customer satisfaction and market share. Contributors to this success included: revamping the sales compensation plan, extensive sales training, joint territory customer calls, creation of a vertical channel support team, development of a select major account program, and enhancing sales tools including the creation of proposal and presentation databases.

**255 W. Howard Street, Suite #1C, Chicago, IL 60610**
**PHONE 312.555.1212 FAX 312.555.1313**
**E-MAIL <u>TBERMONT@BERMONT.COM</u>**

## Todd L. Bermont - Page 2

**EXPERIENCE**

**Midwest Region District Manager (June, 1992 – May, 1994)**

Responsible for selling equipment to a ten state, F1000, MW Territory. Grew MW Territory over 215% in '92 and 320% in '93.

**Yellow XYZ Corporation (July, '89 – May, '92)**

Sold computers and services to a New Business Territory. Increased territory sales over 200% each year on quota.

**Green XYZ Corporation (June, 1986 - July, 1989)**

Sold UNIX computers and DOS PCs to F1000 territory.

**RECOGNITION**

**Red XYZ Corporation**
+ 100% Quota 1992, 1993, 1994, 1995, 1996, 1997, 1998, & 1999
+ Voted "Top Presenting Partner" at 1997 European Sales Meeting
+ Named "Top Instructor" at 1994 European Sales Meeting
+ Won "Top Fortune 1000 Salesperson" Award in 1993
+ Won "Top Team" Award in North America in 1998

**Yellow XYZ Corporation**
+ Five Branch Manager Awards between 1990 and 1992
+ General Manager Award in 1991
+ 100% Club in 1990 and 1991
+ Ranked in the Top 10% of all Employees in 1992

**University of Illinois**
+ Graduated with Honors

**EDUCATION**

University of Illinois, Urbana, IL (1986) - Bachelor of Science, Marketing
Miller Heinmann—Strategic Selling, Conceptual Selling, and LAMP
Acclivus—Coaching and Base Training
Yellow XYZ Advanced Sales School
Green XYZ—Sales School

**REFERENCES**

Available upon Request

**255 W. Howard Street, Suite #1C, Chicago, IL 60610**
**PHONE 312.555.1212 FAX 312.555.1313 E-MAIL**
**TBERMONT@BERMONT.COM**

# SAMPLE FUNCTIONAL RESUME

## Todd L. Bermont

**PROFILE**     Self-employed author, motivational speaker, and sales trainer with over 15 years of executive management and corporate sales experience.

**EXPERTISE**     * Sales Management * OEM and F1000 Key Account Management

* Sales Training * Compensation Plan Design * Increasing Attach Rates

* Territory Management * New Business Development * Interviewing

* Global Business Development * People Development * Hiring

* Project Management * Product Development * Customer Satisfaction

* Cross Selling * Market Share and Competitive Analysis * Negotiation

**EXPERIENCE**     **EXECUTIVE MANAGEMENT**

**President, 10 STEP CORPORATION**

10 Step Corporation specializes in helping companies and individuals succeed through coaching, training, and motivational speaking. Responsibilities include presiding over sales, marketing, accounting, logistics, inventory, investments, publishing, speaking, consulting, and human resources.

**Director, Strategic Partnership Organization, RED XYZ CORPORATION**

Managed global partnerships with leading computer vendors.

Supervised direct reports in US & coordinated additional indirect people in Europe & Asia. Partnerships included a mix of "Buy-Sell" and "Meet-in-the Channel" relationships.

Grew year-over-year sales more than triple the growth rate of Red XYZ.

Additional achievements included increasing attach rates, profitability, customer satisfaction, and market share.

**F1000 Account Channel Manager, RED XYZ CORPORATION**

Managed the Fortune 1000 Channel. Key accomplishments included growing average territory sales over 300 percent, while simultaneously increasing customer satisfaction and market share. Contributors to this success included: revamping the sales compensation plan, extensive sales training, joint customer calls, creation of a vertical channel support team, development of a select major account program, and enhancing sales tools including the creation of proposal and presentation databases.

255 W. Besser Street, Suite #1C, Chicago, IL 60610
PHONE 312.555.1212 FAX 312.555.1212
E-MAIL TBERMONT@BERMONT.COM

## Todd L. Bermont - Page 2

**EXPERIENCE**

**CORPORATE SALES**

**Midwest Region District Manager, RED XYZ CORPORATION**

Responsible for selling equipment to a ten state, F1000, MW Territory
Grew MW Territory over 215% in '92 and 320% in '93.

**Territory Sales Representative, YELLOW XYZ CORPORATION**

Sold computers and services to a New Business Territory. Increased
territory sales over 200% each year on quota.

**Account Sales Representative, GREEN XYZ CORPORATION**

Sold UNIX computers and DOS PCs to F1000 territory.

**RECOGNITION**

**Red XYZ Corporation**

+ 100% Quota 1992, 1993, 1994, 1995, 1996, 1997, 1998, & 1999
+ Voted "Top Presenting Partner" at 1997 European Sales Meeting
+ Named "Top Instructor" at 1994 European Sales Meeting
+ Won "Top Fortune 1000 Salesperson" Award in 1993
+ Won "Top Team" Award in North America in 1998

**Yellow XYZ Corporation**

+ Five Branch Manager Awards between 1990 and 1992
+ General Manager Award in 1991
+ 100% Club in 1990 and 1991
+ Ranked in the Top 10% of all Employees in 1992

**University of Illinois**

+ Graduated with Honors

**EDUCATION**

University of Illinois, Urbana, IL (1986) - Bachelor of Science, Marketing
Miller Heinmann—Strategic Selling, Conceptual Selling, and LAMP
Acclivus—Coaching and Base Training
Yellow XYZ Advanced Sales School
Green XYZ—Sales School

**REFERENCES**

Available upon Request

**255 W. Besser Street, Suite #1C, Chicago, IL 60610**
**PHONE 312.555.1212 FAX 312.555.1212**
**E-MAIL TBERMONT@BERMONT.COM**

# SAMPLE RESUME—ONLINE (ELECTRONIC) FORMAT

TODD L. BERMONT
1255 W. Costa Plente Street
Chicago, IL 60610
(312) 555-1212
tbermont@bermont.com

PROFILE:

Self-employed author, motivational speaker, and sales trainer with over
15 years of executive management and corporate sales experience.

EXPERTISE:

* Sales Management * OEM and F1000 Key Account Management

* Sales Training * Compensation Plan Design * Increasing Attach Rates

* Territory Management * New Business Development * Interviewing

* Global Business Development * People Development * Hiring

* Project Management * Product Development * Customer Satisfaction

* Cross Selling * Market Share and Competitive Analysis * Negotiation

EXPERIENCE:

10 STEP CORPORATION—PRESIDENT (2/00 – Present)

10 Step Corporation specializes in helping companies and individuals
succeed through coaching, training, & motivational speaking.
Responsibilities include presiding over sales, marketing, accounting,
logistics, inventory, investments, publishing, consulting, speaking,
and human resources.

RED XYZ CORPORATION—DIRECTOR SPO (11/95 – 1/00)

Managed global partnerships with leading computer vendors.
Supervised direct reports in US & coordinated additional
indirect people in Europe & Asia. Partnerships included
a mix of "Buy-Sell" and "Meet-in-the Channel" relationships.

EDUCATION:

Graduated with Honors from University of Illinois

REFERENCES AVAILABLE UPON REQUEST

## 4 CS OF AWESOME COVER LETTERS

Once you have created your resume, the next step is to make sure you have an outstanding cover letter. You can have the world's greatest resume, but if you don't have an eye-catching cover letter to go with it, then don't bother sending either.

I'm sure you've heard the saying, "You can't judge a book by its cover." Don't believe it! The flashier and more exciting a book's cover is, the more it sells. Cover letters are the same way. The more interesting your cover letter, the better your chances of getting your resume read.

The cover letter is the "tickler" advertising that gets the reader to want to look at your resume. There are 4 Cs you should remember when writing your cover letter.

---

**4 Cs of Awesome Cover Letters**

1) Concise

2) Customized

3) Creative

4) Close

---

## 1) CONCISE

Much like the resume itself, the cover letter should be short and to the point. Like a powerful advertisement, the copy should be scintillating and grab the attention of the reader.

## 2) CUSTOMIZED

The main difference between the cover letter and the resume is that you add more custom tailoring to the cover letter. In the cover letter you should include references to the company you are interviewing with and how you will be a great asset to them. Stress how your experiences make you the best candidate for the job.

## 3) CREATIVE

For a cover letter to be successful, it must be creative. Think about your key selling points and how they can benefit the company(s) you are targeting. If you are a comptroller and you successfully reduced expenses by 35 percent at your current job, then that may be of real interest to a company that is having trouble containing its costs.

## 4) CLOSE

A successful cover letter will always go for the close. What do I mean by that? In sales, going for the close means asking for the order. The objective of the cover letter is to get you an interview.

### Make sure you end the cover letter
### by asking for the interview!

In summary, cover letters should, be concise and personalized, create interest in you, and ask for the interview. Your cover letters must also convey an understanding of the company and the opportunity, and how you will succeed in the targeted position. On the next page, you'll find an example of an effective cover letter. If you would like more specific guidance, there are many books written specifically on how to generate great cover letters.

January 2, 2004

Mr. I. M. Hipp
Vice President, Customer Service
Rye Bread Company
1 Interviewing Blvd. Suite 310
Danville, CA 94526

Dear Mr. Hipp:

I am applying for the position of Customer Service Manager at Rye Bread Company. As Assistant Customer Service Manager for Baloney Industries, I helped increase customer satisfaction by 40 percent and reduce product returns by 33 percent, all while reducing staff by 10 percent. I accomplished this through fostering teamwork, creating an innovative organization and maximizing call-routing procedures.

I look forward to having the opportunity to meet with you to discuss how I can be an asset to your company.

If you have any questions, please feel free to contact me at (925) 555-1212.

I will follow up on this correspondence next week to schedule a time to meet at your convenience.

Thank you for your time and have a great day.

Sincerely,

Vernon L. Dent

# CREATE A POWERFUL MESSAGE

## CHECKLIST SUMMARY

✔ Compare your **IDEAL JOB DEFINITION** with your **PERSONAL STRENGTHS** and **RESOLVE** any **DIFFERENCES** that could cause you to lose **FOCUS**

✔ **RESUMES** and **COVER LETTERS** are your personal **ADVERTISEMENTS . . . MAKE THEM STAND OUT**

✔ When creating a **POWERFUL** message, **PUT YOURSELF IN THE SHOES OF THE INTERVIEWER**

✔ Use the **10 KEYS TO WRITING POWERFUL RESUMES**

✔ **DON'T PUT COMPENSATION or WEAKNESSES on your RESUMES**

✔ Develop a list of **REFERENCES . . .** and don't forget to ask their **PERMISSION**

✔ Use the **4 Cs TO CREATE AWESOME COVER LETTERS**

✔ In your messages, **USE** industry **"BUZZ WORDS"** to **GRAB ATTENTION**

*"You want to convey an understanding of the company and the opportunity, and how you will succeed in the targeted position."*

# SECRET #5

## WHERE TO FIND JOB OPPORTUNITIES

- **A Complete Job Search Guide**
- **The 15 Best Places to Find Job Leads**
- **Networking**

## A COMPLETE JOB SEARCH GUIDE

Thus far, you have identified your strengths, determined the characteristics you want in a job, and you have created a powerful message that will sell! Great! Now, you have to go out and find interviews.

But where should you look? What follows are the 15 best places to look for job leads.

---

### The 15 Best Places to Find Job Leads
### (Including How to Network)

1) **Local Daily Newspapers and Weekly Business Publications**

2) **National Business Publications**

3) **Internet—Search Engines, Job Portals and Company Web Sites**

4) **Internet—Newspaper Web Sites**

5) **Industry Publications**

6) **Industry Events**

7) **Industry Associations**

---

8) **Industry Tradeshows**

9) **Current Employer**

10) **Job Placement Firms**

11) **College Placement Offices**

12) **Chamber of Commerce**

13) **Job Fairs**

14) **Pink Slip Parties**

15) **Family, Friends, and Acquaintances (NETWORKING!)**

## 1) LOCAL DAILY NEWSPAPERS AND WEEKLY BUSINESS PUBLICATIONS

There are many places to look for an interview. If you ask most people where they begin, they typically start by looking at help-wanted ads in the classified section of their local daily newspaper.

*Local Daily Newspapers* are great resources for finding job opportunities, and are especially good for people who want hourly and entry-level positions.

Higher level positions can also be found in the classifieds when companies are rapidly expanding in, or relocating to, the local area. When companies need to hire a lot of people quickly, classified ads help them get the word out fast.

The most prominent days for help-wanted ads in your local newspaper are Thursdays and Sundays. Usually, these ads are found under the Classified or Job sections.

*Weekly Business Publications* are also useful resources for job leads and company information. Crain's is a publisher that has business publications in many major cities and one of their local publications is Crain's New York Business. Weekly business publications are great resources because they list lucrative job opportunities and provide a wealth of information about the region's business climate.

You will want to read your local newspapers and business publications regularly during your job hunt. You will find the classified ads to be helpful and you will also discover many opportunities by reading stories about the area's companies and economy. Articles about start-up businesses and new locations usually appear far sooner than the help-wanted ads themselves. If you read about a company moving to your city, be proactive and contact them even before they place the help-wanted ads. This will give you an advantage over your competition.

## 2) NATIONAL BUSINESS PUBLICATIONS

National business publications are another means of finding open positions. Publications like The *Wall Street Journal, Barron's, National Business Weekly, Investor's Business Daily* and others often have at least a couple of pages of classified ads for higher level positions.

Typically, the cost of advertising a position in a national periodical is much more expensive than a local newspaper. Thus, companies tend only to post their highest level positions in national periodicals. The higher paying the position, the more difficult it is to find a qualified candidate. As a result, companies often resort to placing national ads because it is more difficult to find top talent.

National periodicals sometimes have regional editions that list local job openings. The *Wall Street Journal* and *Investor's Business Daily* are two such publications. However, if you are looking at a posted position in one of these papers, be prepared to relocate.

I recommend subscribing to one or two national publications during your job hunt. Often, outside of the classified ads, these publications provide great insight into new industries and businesses. You may get some fresh ideas.

## 3) INTERNET—SEARCH ENGINES, JOB PORTALS AND COMPANY WEB SITES

One of the best and fastest growing methods of finding job opportunities is the Internet. Most companies now post open positions through online job portals as well as their own web sites.

To access the Internet, you need a personal computer, network computer or Web/TV device. Plus, you need software called a web browser to allow your computer to communicate with the Internet. I recommend either Netscape or Microsoft Internet Explorer. This software is available at most computer and office supply stores, is downloadable from the Internet, and is typically preloaded on most new computers.

Once you have the access device and software, you need to sign up for an access service. Microsoft Network, Prodigy, AT&T, America Online, and now your local cable TV company provide access services to get to the Internet. Preloaded software on most computers allows you to sign up for many of the services without having to pick up the phone.

If you don't have a computer or access to the Internet from your home, there are still many other ways you can access the Internet. For instance, many libraries have computers you can use for free. Also, most cities have Internet coffee shops and cafés where you can get online for a few dollars an hour.

## How Do You Find a Company's Information Online?

Companies provide information on the Internet through what is called the company's home page or web site. To reach this page, type in the company's Internet address on the address line of your browser. Often, a company's Internet address is either its name or its stock symbol followed by an extension like .com, .org, .biz, or .net. For instance, the address for American Power Conversion is www.apcc.com. This address consists of the company's stock symbol (APCC) followed by the extension. However, Compaq uses www.compaq.com, which is its name followed by the extension.

Just type www and then the company's address (i.e. www.dell.com) on the address line of your browser and you will go directly to the company's home page.

If you are not sure of the Internet address of your targeted company, you can find it with various search engines.

## Popular Search Engines:

- ❏ www.yahoo.com
- ❏ www.excite.com
- ❏ www.northernlight.com
- ❏ www.google.com
- ❏ www.altavista.com

In fact, many of these search engines have their own sections for job openings and postings. However, to find a specific company, type the name of the search engine (i.e. www.yahoo.com) on the address line of the web browser and it will bring up a menu where you can type in search words. At this menu, type in the name of the company and click on the search button. In seconds the search engine will provide you with a list of that company's web sites. Using the computer's mouse, just click on one of the listings and it will take you to the proper web site.

The first page you will see is the company's home page. This page will usually provide an online directory where you will find a wealth of information about the company.

Companies will often post job opportunities in a section of their web site called "employment opportunities."

Also, there are many online bulletin boards, job portals and services on the Internet where you can electronically view job openings and post and send resumes. When this book was printed, some of the most popular sites included www.jobs.com, www.headhunter.net, www.hotjobs.com, www.monster.com, www.jobhunt.com and www.career.com. In addition, there are many "headhunters" and job placement agencies on the Internet. Again, use search engines to find them.

## 4) NEWSPAPER WEB SITES

Many local newspapers have their own web sites that provide you with the ability to search online for jobs. You can search by job category and job location. Additionally, many of these newspaper web sites allow you to post your resume online. Also, these sites provide recent articles and sections on job hunting that give fabulous advice.

## 5) INDUSTRY PUBLICATIONS

Most cities and regions have local publications (newspapers) that are dedicated to different industries or businesses for that area. I call these industry publications. In Chicago one example is *E*Prairie*, a newspaper dedicated to the information technology industry. In St. Louis, the *St. Louis Small Business Monthly* is a publication written for small businesses and entrepreneurs.

Industry publications are tremendous resources for job opportunities. Companies with targeted needs often place job advertisements in these publications. Determine what industries you are interested in and focus on those publications. In addition to local and regional publications, most industries have national and global publications as well.

## 6) INDUSTRY EVENTS

A new venue that is becoming increasing popular among job hunters is the industry event. These events are typically advertised in local and regional industry publications. Industry events are sponsored either by a local trade publication or a company in that industry. These events are designed to foster communication, learning and networking among industry members.

Industry events can provide many job opportunities. You can go to a casual place such as a restaurant or upscale bar and meet counterparts in the industry. Here, you get the opportunity to meet several potential decision-makers, all in one room. Often companies go to these events specifically to look for hiring candidates.

When attending these events, I recommend dressing in business casual and bringing a few copies of your resume. Don't be shy. Usually everyone wears name badges and you can just go up to people and introduce yourself. You will find this environment to be friendly, upbeat and a great place to find job opportunities.

## 7) INDUSTRY ASSOCIATIONS

Joining an association in your field of interest is also another way to meet the "movers and shakers" in your field. Most have monthly meetings where you can meet people via conference calls or in person. Also, many of these organizations bring in high-powered speakers who may know of openings in your field of interest. Besides monthly meetings, many associations have member lists and open job exchanges.

Depending on your field, there may be one or more organizations that you could join. The only downside is that these organizations are sometimes costly. That aside, you can learn a tremendous amount about your field of interest, and these organizations can be full of opportunities.

In addition, you can learn about the latest trends and movements in your industry. Not only will you learn more, but you will also come across as an expert in your interviews.

## 8) INDUSTRY TRADE SHOWS

Trade shows are one of the greatest ways to leverage your time and money to find job opportunities. In one day you can meet dozens of people from the best companies in any given industry. You can learn much about these firms from what they are displaying in the booth. You will enhance your knowledge because you are exposed to the latest industry news. Best of all, you will be one of the only job seekers at the show.

Most industries have both local and national trade shows.

The banking industry has national shows like the Banking Automation show and local shows like the Texas Banker's Association show. The restaurant industry has national shows like the National Restaurant Association Food and Beverage show, and local shows like the Florida Restaurant Association show. The computer industry has shows like COMDEX, NetWorld/Interop and PC EXPO. The retail industry has shows like the National Retail Federation show held annually. Perhaps the most renowned industry shows are the Consumer Electronics and Auto shows.

### How Can You Get the Most Out of a Trade Show?

A great approach is to bring a stack of resumes with you to the show and try to meet as many people as possible. Go to each booth and ask if there is someone who could give you guidance on job opportunities at their company. Leave a resume and get a business card from people you meet.

Then, after the show is over, call them or the people they referred you to, and mention the show. People are much more apt to talk to someone that was referred to them than a person who is "cold off the street." You might get lucky and actually talk with someone at the show that has hiring authority. You never know until you try.

### Develop a Script

Prepare in advance what you want to say as you walk into each booth. Typically, you will only have about thirty seconds to generate interest in yourself, so be prepared. Also, make sure you dress appropriately. If the show is a casual show, like the auto or restaurant shows, then business casual is fine. However, if you are attending a banking show or a healthcare show, you should definitely go with business formal, as dress in these industries is more conservative.

### What Are the Best Times to Attend a Trade Show?

The best times to go to booths at a trade show are during the slow periods between 8:00 am and 9:00 am or between 4:00 pm and 5:00 pm. These are typically the slower times of the show. Also, the final hours of the last day of a show are often slow, as are the times when there are breakout sessions.

Sometimes, going to the show during the booth setup can be advantageous. Often, trade shows do not charge an attendance fee during this time. Here, you can meet the people setting up the booths. During this time it can be more difficult to meet someone who can help you, but you never know. Shows can be quite expensive to get into and admittance is often limited. So, this is a way of accomplishing some of what you want to do without the cost and limitations. During setup, there are no potential customers in the booth, so people are usually more willing to spend time with you.

A key to having successful meetings with people in trade shows is to not bother them when their booths are crowded. You don't want to interrupt them while they are conducting business. This will irritate the potential prospect and limit your chances of success. However, if you go when it is slow in the booth, people are usually eager to talk to anyone if for no other reason than to stay awake.

## 9) CURRENT EMPLOYER

Many people don't realize that sometimes the best opportunities for jobs are often within their own company. You might be thinking, "Come on, I want to get the heck out of here. Why would I want another job at the same place?"

Often, people become dissatisfied in their jobs not because they dislike the company or what they are doing, but because of their boss or situation. Maybe your job just isn't the right fit any more. Maybe the job is stale and you just need a change of pace.

If you have never before taken the time to walk through an "ideal job" exercise (like the one featured in this book), you may not be in the best job, but you may be in the right company. You would be surprised at how much better things can be with a change in management or responsibilities. If you find a job within your company, you don't forgo the vacation time you have earned and the vested time you have accumulated in your retirement and stock option plans.

You can find out about internal job openings in human resource databases, on corporate bulletin boards, and by talking to fellow employees and managers. Sometimes, if you have a good rapport with your manager and he or she wants to see you succeed, you can ask if he or she knows of any new job opportunities.

## 10) JOB PLACEMENT FIRMS

Job placement firms, also called "headhunters," executive recruiters and executive search consultants, are great places to find interviews. There are three types of placement firms. The first type of recruiter is one that is paid solely by the *employer*. Here, the employer pays anywhere from 25 percent to 100 percent of the first year's salary to the search firm to find an employee. The second kind of placement firm is one who charges *you* for the job search. The third type is a hybrid that charges both *you* and the *employer* for their services.

I recommend using the type of recruiting firm that charges the *employer* for their services. However, all are excellent resources.

Make sure you have a good resume before you contact job placement firms. Your resume should be tailored so that the recruiting firm can market you and your skills to their clients. Often, a good recruiter will offer suggestions for your resume. Listen to them because they understand the type of person their client wants to hire and the type of resume that their clients expect.

### Schedule Appointments to Meet
### with the Top Firms in Your Industry

These agencies have dozens of clients looking for employees, and you may be the perfect fit for one of their openings. However, often the top industry specialists may not be located in your city. To find out who these specialists are, and where to find them, look in industry trade publications and talk with friends in the industry. You can also go to many online resources including www.BrilliantPeople.com. Whether or not you are job hunting, it is a good idea to establish a strong rapport with recruiters. They can be very helpful to you throughout your career.

Create a customized sales pitch that you can use at job placement firms. A prepared script is essential because you will have about one minute to sell yourself. If you are not convincing in the first minute, then they will just say, "We have nothing for you." The more prepared and exciting you come across, the greater your chances of being invited to an interview.

## 11) COLLEGE PLACEMENT OFFICES

Another place to find out about job openings is at the job placement office of the college or university you attended. Even if you have graduated, don't hesitate to call the placement office and see what companies are interviewing for positions. Either you or your parents paid a ton of money for your degree from this place. Make them do something for you. If they are not willing to help, try using the potential of future donations as a carrot. Sometimes you can even get a slot on the interview schedule if there are companies interviewing on campus.

If you are still in school, the job placement office is a primary source of opportunities for you. Many schools allow you to submit your resume and bid for interviews. Some hold a lottery and some allow the interviewing firms to pre-select the people they want to interview based on their resumes (again, the importance of a great resume).

### Go to Open Houses

Whether or not you are still in school, a great way to meet companies is to attend open houses that are often held prior to a company interviewing. When I was a student at the University of Illinois, companies such as IBM, Procter & Gamble, Xerox and others held open houses the evening before they interviewed. If you are a graduate or a student who didn't get on the interview list, drop in cold on the open house. Open houses are advertised on campus kiosks, bulletin boards, and in school newspapers.

While you are at it, go to other colleges and universities in your area, even if you never attended those schools. Placement offices are open to the public, so walk in and ask for the schedule of companies coming on campus to interview. Then, look for bulletins on kiosks and in the student newspapers as to what companies are holding open houses.

You have nothing to lose. The worst that happens is you get kicked out of the placement office or a company says they are interested only in current students from that school. But, if you are convincing enough, who knows what can happen?

Once again, I cannot stress enough the importance of creating a script for these scenarios and practicing it. You will only have about thirty seconds to make your impression count.

## 12) CHAMBER OF COMMERCE

Your local chamber of commerce is another great place to go. Here, you can find companies that are relocating to or expanding in your area. These companies hold tremendous opportunity for job hunters. People at the chamber of commerce work with local companies all the time so they may know of an opportunity suited for you.

## 13) JOB FAIRS

One event that became popular in the 1990s and still works today is the job fair. Multiple companies send representatives to job fairs, each searching for candidates for a wide variety of positions. Usually, job fairs are advertised in your newspaper's Local or Business sections, and are typically sponsored by either a newspaper or chamber of commerce.

## 14) PINK SLIP PARTIES

A relatively new kind of networking event that matches job hunters with job seekers is a party called a *Pink Slip* party. This event is similar to a job fair but is informal. For two hours, job hunters and employers mingle in pre-selected circles of ten. Then food and beverages are served and the networking turns into a social event.

These parties started out in the technology field and have spread to other industries as well. They are usually held once every couple of months at a local restaurant or nightclub. Check your local newspapers and web sites to find out the next party near you.

# 15) FAMILY, FRIENDS & ACQUAINTANCES . . . (NETWORKING)

While the previous 14 ideas provide fantastic places to look for a job, perhaps the most effective place you can go is to your family, friends and acquaintances. In many industries, over 80 percent of all jobs are found through networking.

Networking means calling all of your friends, relatives, previous coworkers and acquaintances to let them know you are in the job market. You would be amazed at the number of people you already know who are aware of job opportunities. If they are not aware, at least they can give you the names of people at their companies who may be interested in you or know of appropriate opportunities.

When networking, don't put pressure on your friends and acquaintances by asking them for a job. Instead, describe to them the type of position you are looking for, and the skills you possess. Then ask them if they know of anyone they can refer to you. By the way, always ask people if they can help you. Most people get a natural high from helping others. When you call someone and ask for help instead of asking for a job outright, you are playing off of one of the positives of human nature—the desire to help. Who is going to say, "No, I don't want to help you?"

## Who Should You Call?

Call everyone you know! You never know who might know of a job opportunity. If you have held previous positions, gather all of the business cards you have filed away in a drawer and start calling these people. Also, don't hesitate to call your friends and relatives. There is absolutely NO shame in having someone help you get a job. That is how the real world works and you might as well play along.

Consider other people with whom you have contact on a daily basis. Have you invested before? If so, maybe your stockbroker knows of something. They have many clients who may be aware of opportunities. Other professionals to contact are your insurance agent, your accountant, your doctor, your dentist, and maybe even your hairstylist. These people talk to dozens of people every day and may hear of something. Also, college friends and acquaintances are great sources of job leads—especially those from the same area of study as you.

Don't be afraid to contact these people. After all, most likely you have helped them out in the past, perhaps by giving them business. The least they can do is help you when you need assistance. Make sure you give copies of your resume to each person.

## How Can Your Contacts Help You?

As discussed earlier, many companies have an internal bulletin board with job postings. On their lunch hour, your friends and associates can take a quick scan of the board to see if there are any openings that fit your interests.

Even better, many companies now have an electronic bulletin board with open positions. In fact, one company I worked for had an "Open Positions" database that you could search by position type and expertise. It only takes a couple of minutes for your contacts to scan their company's database to see if there is anything that might be a good match for you.

## Your Friends Can Get Cash $$$ By Helping You!

Many companies offer employees cash rewards for referrals. One company I worked for gave a $500 reward for referring a person to the company if they were hired. So, your friends and associates might not just be doing you a favor; they may be helping themselves.

Besides internal bulletin boards, many positions are in a developmental stage where funding has not yet been approved. If your contacts are at the managerial level, they may have access to position approval databases or they may know of other counterparts who are looking for people. If you can get in before the position is posted, you may have a great shot at that job. At the very least, you may have an edge against future candidates. The bottom line is that networking is a useful tool to finding current job opportunities.

## Finding the Interview Summary

In summary, we have discussed 15 of the best places to look for job opportunities. Some will prove to be more effective for you than others. The key is to decide which methods best fit your personality, then start your hunt. The more effort you put into your search, the better. Your results are usually a direct correlation of your efforts.

# WHERE TO FIND JOB OPPORTUNITIES

## CHECKLIST SUMMARY

✔ There are 15 great places to *FIND* JOB OPPORTUNITIES

✔ NETWORKING and the INTERNET are two of the BEST VEHICLES

✔ When NETWORKING, don't be afraid to ask for HELP

✔ Create Scripts for each NETWORKING and JOB HUNTING SCENARIO

*"You should call everyone you know!*
*You never know who might know*
*of a job opportunity!"*

# SECRET #6

## SELL YOURSELF

- **3 Surefire Methods of Selling Yourself
  to *Get* the Interview**

**F**inding a job opportunity is only half the battle. Now, you need to go out there, promote yourself, and *get* the interviews. Job opportunities rarely just drop in your lap. You need to go out and earn them.

Getting the job you want takes time and dedication.

There are 3 "Surefire" methods to *sell* yourself so you are flooded with interviews. Some of these techniques may fit your personality, while others may not. The key is to try them all and see what works best for you.

---

**3 Surefire Methods of Selling Yourself
to *Get* the Interview**

- **Cold Call for *Known* Job Opportunities**

- **Cold Call for *Informational* Interviews**

- **Direct Market Yourself**

---

# 1) COLD CALL FOR KNOWN JOB OPPORTUNITIES

The first method of selling yourself is cold calling over the telephone, for *known* job opportunities. A known opportunity is where you have identified an actual job opportunity or posting. A cold call is where you are calling someone "out of the blue" who is not expecting your call. This can be an acquaintance or a complete stranger.

If you have identified *(in the 15 Best Places to Find an Interview)* companies that have known job openings, and found someone who could help you, call that person. Don't be afraid. People can't bite you over the phone (and they rarely do in person). Call and introduce yourself. How you introduce yourself is up to you. The key is to relate to the person on the phone with some sort of common ground.

When making cold calls over the telephone, call from your home phone. Make sure you turn off the Caller ID protect feature if you normally have your name blocked. Most companies have Caller ID. If they see your name on the Caller ID they are more likely to answer the phone than if they see *"unknown"* or *"private #"* on their display.

## Before You Call, Write Yourself a Script and Practice It

What? You think that creating a script is too much work?

Well, you will find that by having a script and practicing it, you will be much more comfortable making the call. Cold calling for an interview is just like making a sales call. The best salespeople always prepare for their phone calls and meetings. If you are prepared, you will be successful.

Your script should be very similar to your cover letter. You want to introduce yourself as concisely as possible, create interest in you and then close them for the interview.

**Example:**

"Good morning, my name is _____ and I am hoping you might be able to help me. I noticed your ad for a brand manager position and I was wondering if you are the correct person with whom to schedule an interview?" (Pause for their answer)

**If YES:**

"I currently work for _____company and I have a fantastic track record in bringing new products to market. I saw your opportunity and immediately thought that I could be a tremendous asset to your company. How would I go about scheduling an interview?"

**If NO:**

"Who would you recommend I speak with about this opportunity?"
(Pause for their answer)

Include in your script the hot buttons (areas of interest) and the language or lingo of the company and industry. The best place to find hot buttons are in company mission statements and company annual reports.

When you make your calls, try placing a mirror in front of your phone.

While you are gazing at this mirror, see if you are smiling while talking. People can tell if you are happy, scared, insecure, or somewhere in between by your tone of voice and your energy level—all of which are affected by your nonverbal expressions. Your energy level will be higher when you are smiling and your tone of voice will be more positive. People like talking to positive and energetic people. People don't like helping those who are depressed.

### Getting Rid of the Cold Calling Jitters is Easy!

What . . . you don't believe me? Are you still apprehensive about cold calling? Are you still afraid of picking up the phone and making a cold call? What do you have to lose? The worst that can happen is that the person you are calling can't help you. So what? What is the big deal? If someone says no, are you any worse off than before you asked for help? Of course not!

When cold calling, nine out of ten people may not be able to help you. Don't get frustrated! Look at each individual who can't help as getting you one step closer to a person who can. Be glad they said no, because they just got you that much closer to someone who can say yes. Don't take rejections personally. Cold calling is a numbers game. There are supposed to be rejections. The more people you call, the greater your chances are of reaching someone who might be able to help you.

## 2) COLD CALL FOR INFORMATIONAL INTERVIEWS

An informational interview is where you meet with a person who is in a capacity to hire someone like you, but that person currently does not have an opening. For instance, if you want a position in sales, try to contact sales managers. If you would like a position in accounting, then try to meet with partners in accounting and consulting firms.

Even when managers do not have openings, they are often willing to meet with good candidates because finding good people is always difficult. By talking to you now, they have another prospect to add to their list when a position opens up. Gather up all of your business cards and contact files. You can use these connections in trying to line up some informational interviews. You can also cold call companies to ask whom you should contact. Later, I will give you ideas on how you can use company receptionists to find out with whom you should speak.

Also, look at directories of your graduating classes and social organizations you belonged to such as, fraternities or sororities. Many of these directories list what people are currently doing. Scan through the directories to see if anyone may be in a capacity to hire you.

Once you collect a list of prospects, develop a script and start calling these people. While calling, don't put people on the spot. Just ask them if they can assist you. Tailor your script to the method of how you got the person's name. If you are using a scholastic list, introduce yourself as a graduate of the university or high school. Or, if you are contacting a member of an organization you belong to, introduce yourself as a fellow member.

### Organization Membership Script Example:

"I am graduating from _____ and have an interest in consulting. With the success you have enjoyed in your field, I would greatly value your opinion. I realize that you may not have any openings, but I would greatly appreciate an honest assessment from you about what it takes to succeed in your industry. Could you spare a couple of minutes of your time at some point in the near future? (Pause) When would it be convenient for me to meet with you?"

### Different Industry Script Example:

"Good afternoon, I was wondering if you might be able to help me. I am currently a _____ with expertise in _____. I was wondering if I could get your feedback for a few minutes to see if someone of my background could participate in your industry."

### Same Industry Script Example:

"Good morning, I was wondering if you might be able to help me. I am currently in the market to change positions. I was wondering if you had a few minutes time where I could meet with you and get your feedback on whether or not there would be a fit for me in your company."

Again, the worst the person can say is no, and every no gets you that much closer to a yes.

### Why Spend Time Doing an Informational Interview?

Even though there may be no positions open, when managers spot great talent, they often create a new position just to get the person into the organization. I have done that myself.

In one instance, I once hired someone from a competitor, even though I did not have an opening. I hired this person because he was a great talent and I knew he would be a terrific addition to the team. Plus, he constantly beat my team when we competed with him in the field. I figured if I couldn't beat him, I should hire him.

If the manager can't create a position for you, he or she may refer you to counterparts who do have openings for someone with your talents.

# 3) DIRECT MARKET YOURSELF

In addition to cold calling over the phone, you can do targeted mailings to companies in your field of interest. Here you need an aggressive cover letter that states your desire, skills, accomplishments and credentials. As mentioned earlier, your letter has to be short, to the point and generate interest. The more creative your message is, the better off you will be. With the cover letter, include a copy of your *POWERFUL* resume.

### Try Sending Your Resume and Cover Letter in an Overnight Package

To really get the package noticed, send your information in a Priority pack or Federal Express envelope. Most executives and managers get hundreds of pieces of mail every day, and the only mail that sometimes gets by the gatekeeper (secretary or administrative assistant) is a package that shows urgency—like an overnight package. If you do not have the money to send a priority package, you can improve your chances of getting by the gatekeeper by typing "Personal and Confidential" on the envelope containing your credentials.

### The Fax Machine Can Be Your Next Best Tool

Another way to create urgency is to send a fax to targeted companies. Here you want to try to get attention without advertising to the secretary or administrative assistant that you are looking for a job. To do so, a trick I learned is to have a cover sheet that does not mention the purpose of the fax. Then, on the final page of your fax transmission include a mostly blank page that just says "Thank you for your time." This way your resume and cover letter will be sandwiched in the middle of the transmission and may not be as noticeable to the gatekeeper.

### E-mail Works Too

One other way for you to direct market yourself is to use e-mail. If you are lucky, you may find the name and e-mail address of the right contact person on the company web site. More likely, you will have to send your credentials to a general e-mail address such as info@xyz.com or human.resources@xyz.com.

E-mail is effective because it costs you nothing to send your information and you can blast out your credentials to hundreds of companies at the same time. The downside is that when you send your information to a general address, it often gets deleted.

## To Whom Should You Send These Packages, Faxes, and E-mails?

I recommend sending them to the people who would need your expertise or services. If you are in administration, send your credentials to the director of administration or the administrative manager. If you are in sales, send the resume directly to the sales manager of your local area for that company. Also send a copy to human resources. By sending one to your potential direct line of management and one to human resources, you have two chances of getting noticed. This obviously doubles your potential chance of success.

## It Is Easy To Find Out Who To Target

To find out the names of the people you should send your credentials to, just call your targeted companies and ask. Ask who is the sales manager, administrative manager, human resources manager, etc. You would be surprised how helpful receptionists can be. Start out by being really friendly and respectful to the receptionist. Most people treat receptionists rudely. If you treat the receptionist with respect, they will relate to you better and want to help you more.

## Be Personable

Get the name of the receptionist and call that person by name. People respond much more when called by their name. Thank that person very much for their assistance. You may need their help in the future, so you don't want to take them for granted.

**Example:**

Good morning, how are you today? Who am I speaking with? (Pause) My name is _____ and I was wondering if you might be able to help me? (Pause)

## Be Casual

**Example:**

"You wouldn't happen to know the name of the sales manager in charge of the Southern region, would you?"

In fact, anyone with whom you come in contact can help or hurt your chances of finding a job. It is just good practice to be cheerful and nice to everyone you meet. You never know who might be your ticket to success.

## Sell Yourself Summary

This chapter has discussed 3 Surefire Methods for you to *sell* yourself and *find* job opportunities. In self-promotion, just like in sales, it is impossible to close every deal. The most successful people view each NO as getting that much closer to a YES. Finding interviews is just a numbers game. The more you go out and sell yourself, the greater your chances of success. So once you finish this book, follow the first 5 secrets, then go out there and promote yourself. You will be well on your way to getting the job you want.

# SELL YOURSELF

## CHECKLIST SUMMARY

✔ Cold Call for *KNOWN* JOB OPPORTUNITIES

✔ Cold Call for *INFORMATIONAL* INTERVIEWS

✔ *INFORMATIONAL* interviews are FANTASTIC
ways to DISCOVER OPPORTUNITIES

✔ Direct MARKET YOURSELF

✔ Create SCRIPTS for each METHOD
of SELLING YOURSELF

*"The more you go out and sell
yourself, the greater your chances of success."*

# SECRET #7

## PREPARE

- **4 Steps to Comprehensive Preparation**

**Y**ou searched the 15 best places to find interviews, you went out there and sold yourself, and you have finally *gotten* an interview. Congratulations! Now what?

The first secret to having a successful interview is preparation. By being prepared, you will interview to WIN! While the interview is one of the most exciting aspects of job hunting, it also requires the most energy and preparation.

## 1 MONTH FOR EVERY $25,000

Nothing worthwhile ever comes easy. According to many in the employment industry, job hunting can take up to a month for each $25,000 increment you want to earn. Thus, if you want to make $125,000 in total compensation, it could take you at least five months to find that opportunity ($125,000/$25,000 = 5). That is not to say you cannot do it in less time—in fact, the purpose of this book is to help you achieve your goal in a fraction of the time. However, you should also realize that interviewing is tough work and truly a full-time job.

## JUST AS IN SPORTS, PREPARATION IS IMPORTANT

All successful candidates have one thing in common—they prepare. In sports, teams prepare for hours, sometimes days, watching films of their upcoming opponents. Teams study their opponents' strengths, weaknesses and strategies. Teams practice how to exploit the competition's weaknesses and how to minimize their strengths. Interviewing, just as in sports, requires in-depth preparation. Preparation is often the single most determining factor between those who succeed and those who fail. Only with preparation can you reach your potential.

## IDENTIFY COMPANY STRENGTHS AND WEAKNESSES

You must prepare for the company you are interviewing with by studying its strengths and weaknesses, as well as its corporate philosophies. For example, the company interviewing you may be successful because of their team approach. People may be compensated as a team and motivated by profit sharing to increase productivity and cost effectiveness. In this case, you would want to focus on why you are a great team player and how you have led or motivated teams to success in your previous job.

Conversely, a company may have weaknesses in certain areas. Perhaps they are interviewing you to eliminate one of these weaknesses. Maybe they need more expertise in selling to Fortune 1000 accounts and you have Fortune 1000 experience. Focus on how you can help them by bringing new experience and proven success to the table.

## IDENTIFY THE STRENGTHS AND WEAKNESSES OF YOUR COMPETITION

Additionally, you need to identify your fellow candidates' strengths and weaknesses. In fact, when I interviewed candidates, the most important question I asked was "With all of the great candidates that I am interviewing, why should I hire *you* for this position?"

Maybe there are some people interviewing against you who have more experience. If so, you need to prepare to combat that strength. A potential response is to emphasize your drive, ambition and ability to learn.

## STICK TO THE FACTS

Prepare factual examples from the past that demonstrate your strengths and bring them to life. When I hired employees, I looked for a particular personality, competitiveness, drive and spirit. Even if a person had less experience, if that person fit the personality I desired, I was often willing to take the risk on that person. Many times, I have taken risks believing that, in the long run, a better personality and drive will overcome any shortcomings in experience.

It is important to note that no one is perfect and your competition is no different. Your competition will have weaknesses that you can exploit. Maybe they haven't demonstrated as much success in the past. Maybe their experience isn't as good as your experience. Without being arrogant, make sure you convey your strengths and experience. If you don't "toot your own horn" and sell yourself in the interview . . . nobody else will.

## GO FOR THE WIN!

Interviewing is a mind-numbing task for both parties involved. The person conducting the interview usually has scanned scores of resumes and interviewed several candidates. You, on the other hand, probably have sent out many resumes, made tons of phone calls and went through numerous interviews.

So, how can you turn this long, drawn-out process into one that is rewarding for both you and the interviewer? Make the interview fun, exciting and challenging. Go for the WIN. If you stand out and make the interview a fun experience rather than a stiff one, you will WIN.

## STAND OUT!

Imagine that you are talking to several strangers a day. Who will you remember? You will recall those who are unique and those who leave you with either a very positive or very negative impression. By having fun and being politely forceful, you will leave interviewers with a strong and very positive impression.

Typically, interviewers will ask each candidate the same core questions. They will be looking for specific answers. If you do not answer the first couple of questions with what interviewers want to hear, the interview is over—you have lost! If you are stiff, boring, and seemingly in pain, you will be shown the door, not the job. However, if you are confident, exciting and fun to be around, you will create interest and enthusiasm.

## HAVE FUN!

When I interviewed people in the past, I actually enjoyed many of the interviews. Individuals who were confident in themselves and knew how to have fun were always the most enjoyable to interview. By coincidence, those were typically the candidates I hired.

As an interviewer, I wanted to come out of the interview pumped up! I wanted to be excited about who I was about to hire. Sometimes I was so enthusiastic; I couldn't wait to offer the person the job.

You want to bring interviewers to that point of excitement. If you do, you will WIN!

## THOSE IMPORTANT FIRST MINUTES

Interviewers know within the first couple of minutes if they are interested in you. It is critical in the early stages of the interview to find out what interests interviewers, so you can create a positive first impression.

Imagine playing a game of darts against a solid opponent. Would you play blindfolded? Of course not! Blindfolded, you would not be able to see the target and thus, it would be next to impossible to win the game.

Interviewing is no different from playing darts. If you don't find out what interviewers are interested in early on, you will proceed through the rest of the interview blindfolded. Maybe you'll get lucky and hit a bull's eye, but most likely you will not, and lose the interview.

So, how do you pinpoint targets and keep interviewers interested? The answer is Preparation. Following are the 4 Steps to Comprehensive Preparation.

---

### 4 Steps to Comprehensive Preparation

1) **Research**

2) **Answer the 59 Most Popular Interviewing Questions**

3) **Practice**

4) **Line Up Your Ducks**

---

## 1) RESEARCH

To prepare for your interview, you should do in-depth research on the company, the potential position and if possible, the person who will be interviewing you. Armed with this information, you will demonstrate knowledge, preparation and confidence. You will also discover if the company and position you are interviewing for is right for you. There are multiple sources of information that you can use to effectively research the opportunity. A great place to start is the internet. The Internet is timely, easy to use, and makes information very accessible

### Company Web Sites

Most major companies provide a wealth of information on the Internet through their corporate web sites. Typically, they post information such as their mission statement, financial results, products and services, company history, and even employment opportunities.

## YAHOO! FINANCE

Yahoo! Finance is an awesome site that provides recent news and financial information about public companies and their competition. They offer extensive information about stock performance and analyst recommendations. YAHOO! Finance also has a message board that often provides valuable insight not found anywhere else. You can find YAHOO! Finance by just going to www.yahoo.com and click on the word "Finance" in the media section.

## VAULT

Another Internet site that has recently become increasingly popular is www.vault.com. This site has fantastic general and financial company information, and it also has a message board that employees use anonymously. Employees either vent frustrations or give compliments on this board. I have found many of these conversations on www.vault.com to be unbelievably accurate.

### The Library

In addition to the Internet, the library is another fantastic place to do research. There you have access to company annual reports, *Moody's*, *Standard and Poor's*, *The Wall Street Journal*, *Barron's*, and *Investor's Business Daily*. These are all excellent resources to find information about the company interviewing you and its industry. Just look in the index to find topics of interest.

### Company Receptionists and Investor Relations

Besides the Internet and library, the company itself is a great place to find valuable information. I always find secretaries or receptionists to be extremely helpful. They usually have company information right at their fingertips.

If the company is publicly traded, an even better resource is the investor relations department. Just call and ask them to send you an investor's kit. This kit typically contains the most recent financial reports, press releases and new product brochures, all of which provide valuable information to use in establishing rapport during the interview.

### Call Your Stock Broker

If you can't get through to a company's investor relations department, then brokerage houses are another fantastic place to get similar information. If you have an account with A.G. Edwards, Merrill Lynch, or another full service broker, just call them and ask that they provide you with research reports about the company interviewing you. These reports usually contain detailed information about the company's financials, products and competitors.

## Company Advertisements

Advertisements are beneficial because they show how companies position themselves in the market. An example of positioning is whether the company sells itself as a low cost producer or a high quality manufacturer. Advertisements also give you information on company products and services.

## Local Newspapers

One final place to look for useful information is the local newspaper. You may find a story about the company that could make for a great chance to relate at the beginning of the interview.

## Know More Than Your Competition

The key to successful research is to know more about the company and its industry than your competition. Whether you actually use all of the above sources of information or a small subset, the knowledge you gain will help you succeed during the interview.

## Focus On What is Important

Having all of this great information, what should you know and remember? Focus on company financials, products, target markets (customers), challenges, competition and industry trends.

Is the company a leader in the industry? Have sales increased year to year? Is the firm profitable? What are its best-selling products? What are the profit margins? Is the company conservative or a risk-taker? Does the company have a lot of long-term debt, or do they have cash in the bank? Are there recent government regulations or actions that may have affected the industry?

This information will be extremely useful throughout the interview and makes a great rapport builder. For instance, if you are interviewing for a position at a bank, you could start out the conversation with, "How has the Federal Reserve's action to lower the discount rate affected your deposits?" Or, if you are interviewing for a computer company you could ask, "In such a highly competitive market where computers are becoming more of a commodity, how has your company continued to grow profits while others have failed?"

### Every Annual Report has a Mission Statement . . . Use It!

Companies conduct their operations and form their corporate culture based on the philosophies found in the mission statement. By showing how your skills and talents can help the company achieve their mission, you will convey the message that you will be a valuable addition to the team. For example, the mission statement in a company's annual report provides great insight into company values and beliefs. You can incorporate into the interview how you complement these values, which will also help you establish rapport with interviewers.

## 2) ANSWER POTENTIAL INTERVIEW QUESTIONS . . . (INCLUDING THE 59 MOST POPULAR QUESTIONS)

You have studied the company and you have convinced yourself that you are the most qualified person for this job. You are now ready for the interview, right? No, not quite. You're only halfway through the preparation phase.

The next area of preparation is to anticipate and prepare answers for potential interview questions. You should brainstorm on all of the possible questions you think interviewers will ask during your interviews. Write down those questions and jot down answers to them. Shortly, I will list 59 of the most common types of questions (plus some additional bonus questions) and some sample answers. Use my mock-up responses as a guide to come up with your own answers tailored to *your* strengths. After all, interviewers will be interviewing *you*, not *me*. Let's dive in!

### "Why are you interested in this position?"

**Example:**

"The job description is a perfect match for my skills and aspirations. This is a win-win opportunity where I know I can be successful for your company and that my successes will be rewarded."

This question separates the contenders from the pretenders. Here, a boss wants someone enthusiastic and who is a go-getter. If a person answers this question without conviction, most likely they will not perform well on the job. However, if the person is energetic and gives a well-thought-out response to the question, he or she is a great candidate for the position.

## "What are your strengths?"

**Example:**

"My biggest strength is that I am a team player. Whether it takes a willingness to learn or a willingness to work until 10:00 pm to complete a project, I am going to do what it takes to make the company successful."

This answer should be tailored toward the interviewer's ideal candidate. If the interviewer is looking for someone who is competitive and street-smart, then list those as key strengths. If the interviewer is looking for a team player with proven experience, then focus on those strengths.

How do you know what the interviewer wants to hear? Just ask. At the beginning of the interview you should ask either, "If you had the ideal person for this job, what qualities and characteristics would you want?" or "What are some of the qualities of your top performers?" By asking one of these questions, you will know the areas you should be focusing on during the rest of your interview. However, be prepared to discuss your strengths regardless of whether the interviewer volunteers this information or not.

## "What is Your Biggest Weakness?"

**Example #1:**

"Because I am a team player, sometimes I can work too hard. There are times where I have to learn to step back and relax a little more."

**Example #2:**

"My biggest weakness is that sometimes I work too hard to where my life can get out of balance."

Why should interviewers care about your weaknesses?

This question helps interviewers determine how you will handle difficult situations. You would be amazed at how many people air dirty laundry on this question. I have had people tell me their biggest weaknesses are "dealing with pressure" or "dealing with colleagues" both of those are "no-no's." Every job has pressures and difficult situations.

In addition, the intent of this question is to make you think and to demonstrate your ability to turn a negative into a positive. No boss likes negative feedback. The way this question is answered can tell a great deal about you and whether you could be great employee or a potential problem.

Notice how in the answers above, I turned negatives into *positives* for the company. I know everyone has weaknesses. I have plenty myself. But, I didn't want to hear about these in the interview and neither will your interviewers. Instead, interviewers want to hear a positive response like "working too hard." If you demonstrate the ability to think positively, even in a negative situation, you will score valuable points in the interview.

### "Why do You Feel You are Right for this Position?"

**Example:**

"You mentioned you are looking for someone with proven experience and someone who is motivated. I am ideal for this position because, with my previous experience as _____, I can step in and make an immediate contribution"

This is the ultimate question for you to be able to sell yourself. If you did a good job probing into what the interviewer is looking for in a candidate, you can tailor your answer, go for the close and get the offer.

The interviewer expects you to be confident in answering this question and wants to be sold on *you*, so I recommend being assertive—even borderline aggressive—and proud of your efforts and accomplishments. This is where you can really snag the job.

### "Can you give me the highlights of your resume?"

**Example:**

"During my years as an accountant, I have consistently helped the company reduce expenses, make deadlines and increase efficiencies."

Many interviewers don't have time to study resumes. Typically, the interviewer will have read at least 20 or 30 resumes before getting to yours. At this point, the interviewer's brain starts to get as mushy as instant oatmeal. By asking you for the highlights of your resume, the interviewer doesn't have to reread your resume. This is a great opportunity to sell your talents. You can use the resume as an outline of your credentials.

This question allows you to provide editorial on the most salient points on your resume. Prepare to discuss the key items you think would be most beneficial. Be sure you focus how these areas relate to why you should be hired for the job.

### "Tell me about yourself"

**Example:**

"I am a motivated person who always gives 110 percent and tend to succeed in most everything I do. Whether working or playing a game of golf, I always want to be a winner. I enjoy challenges."

This is the ultimate cop-out question! Interviewers use this question when they are not pre-pared and can't think of anything else to ask. Basically, in asking this question, inter-viewers are trying to figure out how similar you are to them. So in answering the question, you want to provide information that they can relate to and is interesting.

But, *how do you know what will interest interviewers?*

One way to find out is to look at the things in their offices. If they have certificates and awards hanging on the walls, most likely they are very confident and competitive and are looking for someone similar. People like this have egos the size of Texas and it is a good idea to stroke those egos a bit.

If they have subtle furniture and pictures of their family on their desks, they may be more down-to-earth and looking for someone with solid values and a strong work ethic.

Is the office decor modern or old fashioned? Are there fish plaques, sports trophies or article reprints on the wall? These kinds of things give insight into the types of people interviewing you. People hire candidates with similar values, viewpoints, and motivations as themselves.

When answering this question keep your response to two minutes or less. I recommend using the first twenty seconds to provide personal background strengths identified in your personal strength worksheet. The next seventy to eighty seconds should then be focused on personal skills and experiences. The final twenty seconds should be used as a summary where you combine your personal attributes with your work-related strengths.

## "Why did you choose your major?"

**Example:**

I chose marketing because I enjoy working with others and I am motivated by success. Marketing allows me to capitalize on my unique blend of cre-ativity, hard work and ability to learn."

This is an interesting question because it gives insight into how a person thinks. Some have said, "Well, my parents were in this field, so it seemed right." I have also heard answers like, "I wasn't sure what I wanted, and this sounded good." I am constantly amazed at the terrible answers I have gotten to this question. Interviewers look for someone who put thought into this decision and looked years into the future.

Make sure you have a well-thought-out answer to this question. Otherwise, you could knock yourself out of the running.

## "What are your interests?"

**Example:**

"I enjoy playing and watching competitive sports like baseball, football and golf."

I asked this question because I looked for people who thrived on competition for their interests. Competitive individuals usually made very good salespeople. If the person played sports, I asked them if they played for fun or if they played to win. I always looked for someone who competed to win. Other interviewers may look for different interests.

Another interest that is good is traveling, because jobs often entail that. Even casino gambling is acceptable if the interviewer is looking for a risk taker.

You see, you can be honest. However, while sales managers like risk takers, an administrative manager or plant floor manager may not. Thus, make sure your interests are in line with the opportunity.

This question also relates to whether or not you are similar to the people interviewing you. If the interviewer has a golf-ball paperweight on the desk, a picture of Arnold Palmer on the wall, and if you like golf, mention that golf is one of your passions. If the person has several pictures of family on the desk, declare how one of your interests is doing things with the family.

The key here is to answer the question in a way that demonstrates that you've a lot in common with the person interviewing you. However, make sure you are honest! If you don't play golf, don't say that you do. Lying in an interview will always backfire.

## "What are your short and long term goals?"

**Example:**

"My short-term goal is to obtain a position with a company that will challenge me and allow me to grow. One of my long-term goals is to grow with the company and move into management. I feel that in order to be a successful leader, I first have to start out in the trenches. A successful general of any army did not get there by being a desk person all of his life. He got there because he first gained the experience in the trenches."

This question elaborates on your thought process and whether or not you are an employee who can be counted on for the long haul. If your ultimate goal is to become a doctor, but currently you are interviewing for a paralegal position, you probably won't get the job.

However, if you are interviewing to become an accountant and your short-term goal is to perfect your accounting skills while your long-term goal is to be a partner, that makes sense.

## "Tell me how your friends/family would describe you?"

**Example:**

"They would describe me as a competitive person who has a unique ability to succeed. Whether in school, sports or on the job, they would describe me as a person who could always be depended on to give 110 percent and come out ahead."

This is a great way to have people describe themselves from a unique perspective. This question gives valuable insight into how candidates feel others perceive them. It is a very telling question.

## "What interested you in _____ (i.e. chemical engineering)?"

**Example:**

"I have always enjoyed the thrill of solving complex problems and creating new solutions."

Every profession has unique and exciting facets. Otherwise, we would all do the same jobs. What motivates a chemical engineer can be totally different than what inspires another professional.

Having been a sales manager, I looked for people who said in the interview that they were stimulated by money, competition and the thrill of victory. If they didn't say one or more of these things, I would not hire them. Any good salesperson is motivated by money and shouldn't be in the business if they are not.

However, if you are interviewing for a different position than sales, you may need a totally different response. If you are interviewing for a nursing or teaching position and you said that money and competition motivate you, then, most likely, you would be bounced immediately. So customize your responses to the interviewer and targeted position.

## "Using single words, tell me your three greatest strengths and one weakness."

**Example:**

"Competitive, Successful, Creative & Workaholic."

This question forces candidates to be concise and think quickly on their feet. Again, this provides great insight into the mindset of the individual. If you answer this question with multiple-word descriptions, it signals that you did not listen to the question and demonstrates a lack of listening skills. It is my belief, and most interviewers will agree, that if someone is not a good listener, that person will not be a good employee. So if someone asks you to describe yourself using one-word descriptions, answer in single words only.

## "What motivates you to succeed?"

**Example:**

"Seeing a challenge and conquering it."

Motivation is key to success for any job. If the motivation does not fit what the interviewer is looking for, then there is a mismatch. Make sure your motivation is in line with what the interviewer would expect for the job.

## "What is your ideal job?"

**Example:**

"My ideal job is one that utilizes my talents to the fullest and allows me to grow and be rewarded as I contribute to the success of the organization."

Here, the candidate should state aspects of the job at hand. If the candidate's idea of the ideal job does not match the job at hand, then the interviewer will know the candidate will not work out and move on to the next interview.

## "What traits do you look for in an ideal company and an ideal job?"

**Example:**

"I want to work for a company that does not tolerate mediocrity, and a company that is growing, profitable and an industry leader like yours. I want a job that is challenging and where I can make an immediate contribution"

The person interviewing should state the qualities of the company and the job at hand. If there is a match, then that is great. If not, it's on to the next candidate.

### "What qualities do you feel are important to be successful in _____ (i.e. customer service)?"

**Example:**

"A successful customer service representative has to be a resourceful, a quick-thinker and a problem-solver."

Here, you want to be able to articulate what the interviewer feels is important to succeed. There are many right answers to this question and it depends on the job and the personality of the interviewer. Be truthful with yourself and your interviewer. Believe it or not, interviewers can usually see right through the BS. For instance, if a shy and reserved person told me the keys to success were to be outgoing and gregarious, I immediately saw a red flag and flushed the candidate because they did not exemplify what they were saying. Don't ever lie.

### "What previous experience has helped you develop these qualities?"

**Example:**

"On my previous job as an _____(i.e. administrative assistant), often I had to work with irate customers when my boss was not around. As a result, I was forced through the school of hard knocks to learn how to ease customer tension and make quick decisions to protect valuable customer relationships."

If you do not have previous Position-Relevant Experience, then relate some other experience that could demonstrate skills necessary for the job. An example could be as farfetched as convincing a date to go to a hockey game over a movie. That would demonstrate selling skills. For an accounting job, you could mention how you were the treasurer for a club at school or that you handled the finances of your condominium association.

Those I interviewed who admitted that they had no position relevant experience, and could not come up with any experiences that could somehow relate to the opportunity at hand, were immediately disqualified. Good employees have to think quickly on their feet. If a candidate did not provide an answer to a question in a timely and sincere manner, I would immediately reject that person.

## "Can you give me an example of teamwork and leadership?"

**Example:**

"As project leader, for _____(i.e. final assembly team) I held a contest to see who could come up with the best idea to improve quality. This resulted in everyone providing valuable feedback and feeling they were a part of the team, and perhaps most importantly reduced defects by 15 percent."

In most positions, teamwork is critical to success. Typically, people want team players. In fact, I usually wanted the best of both worlds when I hired someone. I looked for a team player, yet I also wanted someone who competes to win on an individual basis.

Be careful in your answers, though. You don't want the interviewer to think you are too dependent on others, yet you don't want them to think you are too independent or a wild duck either. The key is to demonstrate that you possess both talents and that you can go with the flow.

## "What was your greatest challenge and how did you overcome it?"

**Example:**

"My greatest challenge was handling a very emotional employee. I overcame this challenge by finding out what motivated her and discovering how to channel her emotions into positive results. I found that all I had to do was to simply tell her each day how much I appreciated her efforts and how valuable she was to the team. As a result her performance substantially improved."

This question provides insight on how tested a person has been, and what that individual perceives to be a big challenge. This question really separates the good from the mediocre. Poor candidates have a tough time thinking of a challenge and are weak in their answers.

I looked for a tough and thought-provoking challenge, one where the person had to think beyond the bounds to solve. If someone brought up a weak challenge as being a big deal, I lost interest quickly.

## "Have you received any special recognition?"

**Example:**

"One accomplishment is that _____ I made the Dean's List."

When I interviewed candidates, I did not settle for mediocre people. I expected someone to have received some sort of recognition.

Recognition can be anything from making the Dean's List to 100% Clubs to raising money for a charity. If someone can demonstrate an ability to achieve special recognition, most likely, that person will be a good employee.

If you have not been recognized for your efforts, then do something to gain some sort of recognition. This can be as simple as volunteering to help with a charitable function or volunteering to be a mentor to a child. Or, you can do what I have done and call your local school district and offer to be a guest lecturer or teacher. Teaching kids is fun and rewarding. I have developed a tremendous respect for teachers after volunteering to teach.

### "Why should I hire you over the other candidates I am interviewing?"

**Example:**

"Because of my competitiveness, proven success and unique ability to learn, I will make an immediate contribution to the continued success of your organization. Your company already has enough risks every day—why risk hiring someone who is less than the best? I know I will make you proud to have hired me."

When I asked this question, I wanted the person to be a bit cocky. This is where the person can really go for the close. (Since I hired for sales, I looked for people who were "closers.") I also looked for them to repeat some of the traits I noted were important during the interview. That showed good listening skills.

### "Do you have any questions?"

To answer this question you should ask questions that demonstrate thought and creativity.

**Example #1:**

"How do you reward top performers?"

**Example #2:**

"Is there a cap on earnings for top performers?"

Questions like these exude confidence. These assumptive questions illustrate that you are a positive individual, you are willing to go for the close, and show that you are confident you will be offered the job.

Top candidates always ask at least a couple of assumptive questions.

If candidates didn't ask questions during the interview, or if the questions asked were not thoughtful, I usually rejected them. I looked for thought-provoking questions. I expected questions about company strengths, employee turnover, benefits, visibility for top performers . . . etc.

## "What did you earn last year?" and "What are your compensation expectations?"

Both of these are very difficult questions to answer and you must be very careful. If you give too much information, you will paint yourself into a corner when it comes to salary and compensation negotiations. I suggest using ballpark figures.

### Question #1 Example:

"Last year, I was in the ballpark of the middle 100s"

### Question #2 Example:

"My expectation is that I am compensated at a level commensurate with my expertise and proven track record, and at a level comparable to similar positions elsewhere."

## Bonus Questions

What follows are some additional questions you will likely see in your interviews. I am not going to provide you with the answers to these questions because I want you to exercise your mind. It has been said, "If you give a man a fish, you feed him for a day . . . if you teach a man to fish, you feed him for a lifetime." Taking this into account, I want you to start preparing on your own.

Answer these questions positively and with confidence. For example, the first question is:

### "Why are you looking to leave your current position?"

### How TO Answer:

"I am at the stage in my career where I want a job that is more challenging and rewarding."

### How NOT to Answer:

"I am leaving because I hate my boss and my company is full of losers."

Also, do not provide any proprietary information about your current or previous jobs. Unfortunately, some companies interview people from the competition just to gain proprietary knowledge and not because they are actually considering hiring you.

Plus, interviewers will look negatively upon you if you provide them with information that you should not give. More important, providing confidential information is unethical. Proprietary or confidential information can be something as simple as telling them how many shifts a factory is running to the cost of goods or the number of people in your division.

Try not to provide specific numbers. Instead, try to focus on percentages like increased sales 120 percent in my territory or reduced the cost of production by 33 percent.

### General Questions:

General questions are a way to get general information about your thought process.

1) "Why are you looking to leave your current position?"

2) "What was your greatest accomplishment at _____company?"

3) "How does your company compete against ours?"

4) "Have you ever been asked to do something unethical? If yes, how did you handle it?"

5) "What do you do if you totally disagree with a request made by your manager?"

### Leadership Questions:

Leadership questions give insight into your leadership skills.

1) "When in a group setting, what is your typical role?"

2) "How do you motivate a team to succeed?"

3) "Have you ever had to fire anyone? What caused you to take this action?"

4) "Have you ever held a leadership role? How did you motivate people in that role?"

5) "What was your most difficult situation? What did you learn from it?"

### Teamwork Questions:

Teamwork questions give insight into how you work as part of a team. In today's environment, most managers feel it is critical to hire team players.

1) "How do you feel about working in a team environment?"

2) "Describe to me how you helped the morale of the team and motivated them to succeed?"

3) "Have you been in team situations where not everyone carried their fair share of the workload? If so, how did you handle the situation?"

## Problem-Solving Questions:

Problem-solving questions demonstrate your ability to come up with solutions to difficult situations and your ability to think on your feet.

1) "Can you give me an example of a difficult work situation and how you handled it?"

2) "How do you prioritize when you are given too many tasks to accomplish?"

3) "Why are manhole covers round?" I know this question sounds crazy, but one of my previous managers used to always ask it. Later in this book I will tell you how to handle this question, but first, try it on your own.

## Drive and Motivational Questions:

Drive and motivational questions are a way to understand how motivated you are and what "makes you tick."

1) "Tell me about one of your most significant accomplishments."

2) "What was your favorite job and why?"

3) "What have you done to make yourself more proficient in _____?"

## Organizational and Planning Questions:

Organizational and planning questions demonstrate how you approach your job and how you think. If someone appears disorganized, more likely than not, that candidate will be rejected.

1) "Do you set goals for yourself? If so, how?"

2) "Tell me about a goal you set for yourself and how you accomplished it."

3) "How do you go about your workday?"

4) "Do you typically achieve what you set out to do?"

## Miscellaneous Questions:

1) "What would your last boss say were the areas that you needed to improve upon?"

2) "What de-motivates or discourages you?"

3) "Do you work better in teams or by yourself?"

4) "How important to you is a positive attitude?"

5) "What is your definition of success?"

6) "What was your biggest disappointment in your prior position?"

7) "What do you feel it takes to have a successful career?"

8) "What do you like the most about your current position?"

9) "What do you like least about your current position?"

10) "What do you want to do in five years?"

11) "Tell me about the most difficult decision you have had to make."

12) "Can you explain why you were not employed during _____ period of time?"

13) "Why did you choose to go into _____ industry and/or _____ company?"

## Now Comes the Fun Part

You need to answer each of these questions in your own words. I have given you examples and techniques of how you can answer these questions. Tailor your answers to your areas of interest, and to your personality and strengths.

These questions are either questions I have been asked myself or questions I liked to ask when I interviewed other people. Your actual experience will vary. However, going through these questions should be helpful in your pursuit. Some industries and occupations will dictate more specific questions, but I guarantee that you will hear at least a couple of these questions in your next interview.

When you write down answers to these questions, I suggest that you jot down a couple of key words that will help you remember how you want to respond to each inquiry. By answering each possible question before the interview, you will be prepared for almost any situation.

So, spend a few moments taking another look at the questions, and answer them as if you were in the interview. Mold the answers to your skills, experience and personality.

## Be Flexible In Your Answers

Be able to adapt your answers to any situation. People hire people who they like and who are like them. You want interviewers to be able to relate to you on both a professional and personal level. That is why it is so important to develop a strong rapport with interviewers.

So, if you leave enough flexibility in your answers, you will be better able to relate to any-one you meet. Interviewers are much more inclined to offer you a job if you have developed a positive rapport.

# 3) PRACTICE

At this point you may be feeling a bit overwhelmed. I know that seeing a stream of questions can be frustrating. But you would be surprised at how easy it is to prepare once you dive in.

The more prepared you are, the more confident you will be, and the better you will perform in the interview. However, before I leave this topic, I cannot neglect to mention the most crucial part of preparation—PRACTICE.

### Get a Friend to Help

I recommend getting friends to help you practice. Have them play the role of the interviewer. Do not use your family. They will be too easy on you. You want the role player to be someone who will not hesitate to provide objective feedback and criticism when necessary.

Give the role player the list of possible questions you developed as a result of our anticipating questions exercise. Then, act out the interview as if it were for real. Afterwards, make sure you get feedback. Tell your friend not to be afraid to be critical . . . Better to bomb out with your friend than the interviewer!

Practice the interview until you are confident you can get the job. Make sure you start the role-play by knocking on the door and entering the office or room. Do not break out of your role this will hurt your concentration and will not properly simulate the interview. After the interview, you can go over how you performed.

### Record Your Performance

Another great way to review your practice is to record yourself using audio or videotape. By listening to yourself on tape or viewing yourself on video, you can really identify your strengths and weaknesses. Maybe you say the word "uh" once every ten words. If you have a video, you might notice poor posture or a bad habit like wiping your brow or scratching your nose. By recognizing a weakness in practice, you can work to overcome that weakness prior to the interview. The more you practice and prepare, the better you will do in the interview.

### You Can Never Practice Too Much

Professional golfers will hit buckets of balls every day to continue to improve and perfect their skills. In fact, I have heard that Tiger Woods sometimes even practices after finishing a tournament. Work on perfecting your skills daily. This can be done even as you are driving your car. Talk out loud to yourself and practice your answers. You will be amazed at how this will sharpen your skills.

### Try Practicing In Front of a Mirror

Believe it or not, I have been known to practice for hours in front of a mirror. By looking in the mirror, I can work on my smile, posture, attitude and appearance. It is amazing how much I learned about myself in doing this exercise. Try practicing in front of a mirror yourself and see how your skills will improve.

## 4) LINE UP YOUR DUCKS

Okay, now you are thoroughly prepared for the interview. You have researched the company, perfected your answers to possible questions, and you have practiced. You are almost there. But, there a few more things you need to do.

### Get the Correct Spelling and
### Pronunciation of the Person(s) You Will Meet

Correct spelling is imperative for thank you notes, and proper pronunciation is essential during the interview.

### Get Directions on How to Get to the Interview

If you get lost and end up being late, you will give a poor first impression. You can get directions from many online spots. YAHOO! has a great maps section on their web site. You can also call the company receptionist for directions. Make sure, though, that you have the correct address. Don't just go by what is in the phone book. I have a friend that once went to the wrong location because the company moved. Needless to say he missed the interview and lost the job opportunity. Confirm the address!

### Pick Out Your Interview Clothes Ahead of Time

By planning ahead, you can concentrate solely on the interview. You do not want to panic on the day of your interview because your favorite interview suit is at the cleaners.

### Plan to Show Up Early

Arrange your schedule so you can show up for the interview ten to fifteen minutes early. You can never look bad by being a few minutes early. However, being late to an interview will kill your chances of success. If you plan on being late, then you might as well chew garlic before the interview, too. Being early gives you the chance to either get extra face time with interviewers or additional time to learn more about the company and its culture. I have always been fascinated by how much you can discover just by talking to the receptionist and observing how employees interact with each other. So, make sure you show up a little early to create that positive first impression.

# PREPARE

## CHECKLIST SUMMARY

✔ It can take up to 1 MONTH for every $25,000 YOU WANT TO EARN

✔ TREAT the JOB HUNT like a JOB

✔ Identify the STRENGTHS and WEAKNESSES of the COMPANY interviewing you and of YOUR COMPETITION

✔ ANSWER the 59 most popular interviewing QUESTIONS

✔ PRACTICE your interviewing skills DAILY

✔ Line up your DUCKS

*"Interviewers know within the first couple of minutes if they are interested in you."*

# SECRET #8

## TRAITS OF IDEAL CANDIDATES

● **8 Traits Interviewers Expect of Ideal Candidates**

**A**re you ready for the interview? If so, you've finished the most tedious and difficult undertaking—the preparation and psyche-up. The next secret to a successful job hunt is to know the type of person and characteristics that interest interviewers. Being able to identify what interviewers are looking for will help you perfect your answers and position yourself during the interview. Later in the book, I will teach you how to identify exactly what interviewers want in their ideal candidates. But, for now, I will cover 8 traits interviewers look for in an ideal candidate.

---

### 8 Traits Interviewers Expect of Ideal Candidates

1) **Confident**

2) **Organized**

3) **Personable**

4) **Conscientious**

5) **Efficient**

6) **Creative**

7) **Goal-Oriented**

8) **Problem-Solver**

---

## 1) CONFIDENT

Interviewers want people who are confident about themselves and their skills. If you do not feel confident and excited about yourself, then how are interviewers supposed to believe in you? Experience breeds confidence. If you lack experience, you can make up for it in preparation, enthusiasm and drive.

Envision going to a restaurant and asking the server if the fish is good. If he says, "Well, some people like it, but I've never tried it," you may be hesitant to order the fish. However, if he says, "The fish is fantastic and it's one of our most popular dishes," you may be more inclined to order it because the server is so confident about the dish.

Interviewing is much the same. Confidence instills excitement in you and your skills. If you are excited about yourself, you will convey that enthusiasm. Everyone wants someone who is enthusiastic.

Once or twice a day, remind yourself that you are FANTASTIC! Tell yourself that you have qualities that no other person can match. We are all human and no two people are exactly the same. So celebrate! You have something no one else has—your unique individuality. You have to believe that only you can be hired for the job. With your qualities, experience, individuality and enthusiasm, how can any company go wrong?

So many people look at life as if the glass is "half empty," rather than "half full." A positive attitude will help you not only in interviewing, but also in life. Again remember, you are great! You have a tremendous amount of talent and enthusiasm. You will succeed. Continue to tell yourself that you will thrive, and you will believe it. Most importantly, you will believe it because it is true!

## 2) ORGANIZED

Nothing is more annoying to interviewers than a person who appears disorganized. Once again, you need to be prepared. Do not hesitate to write down some notes prior to the interview. Jot down some topics you want to cover and questions you want to ask. An interview is like an open book test—you will not be thrown out of the interview for looking at your notes. Notes are perfectly acceptable. In fact, bringing notes shows forethought and preparation.

One trick I used during interviews was to write down in small print a few notes on key topics and questions I wanted to discuss. In case I was nervous, I always wrote the name of the company and person I was interviewing with on the top of the page so I wouldn't forget them.

I would then keep my notebook open during the interview. Don't be shy. It is perfectly acceptable to take notes during the interview. No one expects you to have a perfect memory. And if they do, then who wants to work for a company like that?

Note taking can be useful as long as it doesn't distract from the interview. If the interviewer says a few phrases that you want to take note of by all means write them down. Taking notes shows your interest in the position and the organization—just do so in moderation.

## 3) PERSONABLE

Smile. "When you smile, the whole world smiles with you." This popular sentiment is so true. In smiling, you create a friendly atmosphere that is more pleasant for both you and your interviewers. As a result, interviewers will be more attentive. The more you smile, the more you will succeed.

Again, think of going to a restaurant. Imagine one day you have a waitress who is a grouch, and everything she does seems to be an effort. Then, another day, you have a different waitress, who is cheerful, and concerned about how you enjoyed your meal. Which meal would you enjoy more? To whom would you give a good tip?

Interviewing is similar. Interviewers are inundated with prospects. They remember people who smile, who are genuinely pleasant, and who enjoy the interview. If you are not friendly during the interview, your chances of getting the job will be slim.

Interviewers want employees who are a pleasure to be around. If you are friendly and you get along well with interviewers, you will be viewed as a positive person—one who would be an asset to companies.

However, if you are frowning and down . . . who wants to see that every morning? Not being friendly is the quickest way to get an interviewer's heel on your behind. Be friendly and personable and you will succeed.

## 4) CONSCIENTIOUS

I have never been in an interview yet where the person interviewing me has wanted a lazy bum for the job. Do not—I repeat, do not go into an interview and say, "I am looking for a 9 to 5 job." Forget it. Everyone wants a hard-worker. Even if you don't want to work long hours, please don't say that in the interview. Interviewers want to hear that you are flexible and that you are willing to work the hours necessary to get the job done.

Interviewers might ask, "Are you willing to work long hours?" To answer, you might want to say, "I am willing to spend whatever time it takes to finish the job. In some cases that might be accomplished in a normal work week, and in other cases, it might take longer."

Or, interviewers could ask, "Are you looking for a straight 9 to 5 job?" A response to this question would be, "I am looking for a position that is challenging and best utilizes my skills more than a position that is just a 9 to 5 job."

The point I am trying to get across is that employers look for hard-workers. You will be able to decipher on your own, how long and hard you will have to work in a particular job. If the position is not for you, then you can always turn down the offer.

In today's job market, you will be competing with young, aggressive and motivated people who are enthusiastic and willing to work long hours. You need to convey these same traits. Otherwise you will not succeed.

## 5) EFFICIENT

In addition to wanting conscientious employees, employers want employees who will work smart and efficiently. Some people will take ten hours to complete the same amount of work that others might complete in two. Employers want people who will put in a full day's work, but they do not want people who will work hard and get nothing accomplished. They want efficiency.

## 6) CREATIVE

Whether you are interviewing for a position in marketing, accounting, computing, or a job on the plant floor, 90 percent of job interviewers favor people who demonstrate creativity. Creativity demonstrates the ability to think on your feet and dream up better methods of accomplishing objectives.

### What If You Are Not Creative?

You might be thinking, "I'm not a creative person. Does that mean I can't get a job?" First of all, everyone is in some way creative. Secondly, creativity is not a "show stopper" in itself, but expressing creativity sure helps.

### Just By Being Human You Demonstrate Creativity

For example, do you dress or part your hair the exact same way as everyone else? No! You look the way you want to look . . . and that is creative. Anyone can look at a position from its job description alone. The way you differentiate yourself is by exploring those areas of the position to which you can add your own definitions and perspectives.

Say that you are interviewing for a claims adjuster position at an insurance company. The standard job description is that you inspect cars that were in accidents, assess the damage, and negotiate a settlement with the customer. You, being the creative person you are, could demonstrate creativity by expanding the job description.

**Example:**

"Not only am I qualified for your position, but, with my background, I can help streamline the process, improve customer satisfaction and save the company money."

Super! By being creative, you have eliminated half of the people interviewing for the position. You demonstrated a talent that others did not. You showed an ability to understand and streamline processes as well as a desire to make the customer happy. The previous candidates did not demonstrate the expertise you just stated. Now, everyone who interviews after you must articulate that they have these qualities. You just raised the bar on your competition!

### Even in the NBA, Creativity Is Important

In basketball, Michael Jordan succeeded because he was able to set himself apart from his competition. Early in his career, he became known for his relentless attacks to the basket, his dunking skills and his power. As he got older, Michael realized the competition was starting to get wise to his moves and that he no longer had his former speed and stamina.

Instead of relying on his old tactics, Michael re-invented himself by developing an incredible fade-away jump shot that was almost impossible to defend. Michael's creativity allowed him to excel against the toughest competition in the NBA. You, too, can differentiate yourself to be creative and WIN!

## 7) GOAL-ORIENTED

Today's labor force is better trained and more productive than ever. Most often, the one trait that can separate the superstars from the rest of the pack is whether or not you are goal-oriented.

What does it mean to be goal-oriented? It means you have a reason for existence; you aren't following the pack, you are leading it. Having goals means you know what you want out of your career, your relationships and your life. If you set goals, you will be more successful. Ask the top performers in any profession, and they will tell you that the main reason for their success is they set aggressive, yet achievable, goals.

### Think About What You Want In the Future

Interviewers will ask questions like, "Where do you want to be in five years?" or "What are your career aspirations?"

This is a good time to think about what you want to achieve. Without set goals and objectives, you will be relegated to the second team. Do you want to go into management? Do you want to earn big money? Do you want to travel? Do you want to help others?

What are your goals and aspirations? Take a few minutes now to write down a couple of ideas. The best thing about goals is that they need not be written in stone. You can always choose to achieve more or change your existing ones. The key is having something to look forward to in the future. When you stop looking forward, you have no reason to live. I have known of many people who died within weeks of their retirement! Scary, huh?

By having specific goals that are aggressive and rewarding, you will be viewed positively by those who are interviewing you!

## 8) PROBLEM-SOLVER

Companies want more from employees than someone who shows up just to punch a clock. Employers now expect their workers to be problem-solvers. Whether it is someone on the plant floor or a supervisor, companies are looking for their employees to assist in solving problems and to come up with new ideas to streamline processes. Some employers even offer incentive bonuses to employees who generate recommendations that save the company money. Demonstrating qualities in the interview that show you are a problem-solver will give you an edge in your interviewing.

# TRAITS OF IDEAL CANDIDATES

## CHECKLIST SUMMARY

✔ Be CONFIDENT, ORGANIZED,
  PERSONABLE and CREATIVE

✔ Once or twice a day, remind yourself
  that YOU ARE FANTASTIC!

✔ The more you SMILE, the more you
  will SUCCEED

✔ Exemplify the traits of a CONSCIENTIOUS
  and EFFICIENT WORKER

✔ Demonstrate that you are GOAL-ORIENTED
  and a PROBLEM-SOLVER

✔ WRITE down some of your GOALS
  and ASPIRATIONS

*"Having goals means you know what
you want out of your career . . . and your life."*

## SECRET #9

# HOW TO HAVE A SUCCESSFUL JOB INTERVIEW

- **The 3 Keys to Successful Interviewing**
- **The 6 Phases of a Successful Job Interview**

**W**elcome to the INTERVIEW, one of the most exciting aspects of the job hunt! In this chapter, I will cover the 3 Keys to Successful Interviewing. These keys will serve as the foundation for interviewing. I will also discuss The 6 Phases of a Successful Job Interview. These phases define the structure and provide a step-by-step approach to ultimate job interviewing success.

---

### The 3 Keys to Successful Interviewing

- **Positive Mental Attitude**
- **Dress For Success**
- **Have FUN**

---

## POSITIVE MENTAL ATTITUDE

Maintaining a positive mental attitude is crucial to having a successful job interview. No matter what I say in this chapter, if you do not feel good about yourself going into the interview, all of your preparation will be for naught. If necessary, read Secret #1 again and remember that you are a GREAT person!

Imagine for a moment that you're shopping for a television set. You go to Shemp's TV Emporium and the salesperson walks up to you and says, "May I help you?" You say you're just looking. Five minutes later, you ask the salesperson what the twenty-four inch RCA TV costs. The salesperson walks slowly behind the counter, fumbles through the price lists, and coldly says, "That model sells for three hundred dollars . . . do you want to buy it?"

Next, you go to Curly's Electronics. While, you are looking at the same twenty-four inch RCA TV, the salesperson walks up to you and says with a smile, "Isn't that a great TV? The picture is awesome and the manufacturer is top of the line. We never see any coming back for repairs. What kind of TV are you looking for?"

After talking with her for a few minutes you ask her how much it costs. She says, "This unique model sells for only three hundred and ten dollars and if you ever have a problem with the TV, we can service it right here. If you would like, I can have one of our service representatives deliver it to your home and set it up for you."

I don't know about you, but I would buy the TV at Curly's—even though it costs ten dollars more. I would buy it there because of the salesperson's knowledge and even more so, because of her positive attitude.

## Interviewing Is Selling

The reason I make analogies between selling and interviewing is because interviewing is selling! In an interview, you want to have a positive attitude so you will get the job. One way to convey an energetic attitude is to be enthusiastic about the job. Go in there and act as if the job is the best thing that could ever happen to you and that you are the best thing that could ever happen to the company. Communicate that the best decision the company could make is to hire you.

## Make Interviewers Feel Good

Make interviewers feel good about themselves, their companies, and the opportunities offered.

**Example:**

"I just want to let you know how much I appreciate you taking your valuable time to meet with me. This position sounds so exciting and your company is the leader in the industry."

## Be Assertive

Be assertive about yourself. If you don't speak highly of yourself, nobody will.

**Example:**

"I would be great in this position. With my ability to solve problems and my ability to learn, I could immediately make a contribution to your firm."

### You Are Equal

When you are interviewing, it is important to realize that you are equal to the person interviewing you. If you put interviewers on a pedestal, you will be nervous and timid. You have as much choice in this process as they do. After all, you are the one choosing to attend this interview. An interviewer may want to hire you on the spot, but you might not like the company and choose not to accept. The most successful employee/employer relationships are those based on mutual trust, respect and equality. When you view yourself as an equal, you will perform at your peak both in the interview and on the job.

### Personal Mantra

Be confident, have fun and, most of all, be positive about the contribution you can make! Use the ideal job mission statement you created as your personal mantra. Believe in your destiny and you will achieve it. The worst that happens is you get bounced from the interview. So what? If your mission is your destiny, then one rejection will not stop you from achieving it.

Having a positive attitude will give you every chance to succeed in the interview!

## DRESS FOR SUCCESS

When you knock on the door, the first thing interviewers see is your appearance. Whether you are dating, job interviewing or meeting someone for the first time, first impressions are always important. 90 percent + of all communication is nonverbal. You want to look good . . . it definitely has a major impact on your chances of getting a job.

Seldom will the way you dress actually get you a job. However, if you do not wear the appropriate attire during the interview, you could easily lose one. Whether you interview for an administrative job or for vice president of a major corporation, dress professionally.

Why is the way you dress so important? Think of flying. If you see the pilot wearing torn blue jeans and a stained white T-shirt, would you feel comfortable flying on that plane? Or, would you rather fly with a pilot wearing a clean, freshly pressed blue uniform?

Interviewers would rather fly with the pilot wearing the uniform. The way you dress demonstrates the kind of person you represent. If you are clean-cut and professional looking, you will make a far greater first impression than if you look like you just walked out of a racetrack. Don't forget people remember what they see much more than what they hear. "A picture is worth a thousand words"? Need I say more? *Dress professionally!*

## Dress For Success—Men

### Business Suits

For men, professional attire includes a conservative, well-tailored suit. The suit should be blue, gray, black, or charcoal. The suit should be solid or feature a subtle pattern. Loud pinstripes or bold plaids look great at banquets, but not at interviews. The suit fabric should be mostly, if not 100 percent wool. A small touch of another material can help keep the suit's shape, but should be limited to less than 25 percent of the total suit's composition.

### Shirts

Wear a good shirt. The shirt should always be white and nicely starched. You can never go wrong with a white, long-sleeved shirt. If you want to wear a blue shirt, save it for when you go bowling, not interviewing. Short-sleeved and colored shirts are less formal and not appropriate in the business setting. Save your short-sleeved shirt for the poker room.

### Ties

The tie should be conservative. The best styles are traditional striped, geometric and paisley.

### Shoes

Make sure your shoes are shined and in good condition. Interviewers will look at whether or not you have shined shoes. Shined shoes present a professional image and demonstrate a good work ethic. If you wear shoes with holes in the sole, you'll convey a negative image.

### Socks

One of the things that men often overlook, are their socks. I have seen men walk into interviews with cleanly pressed suit and shined shoes, but mismatched socks. To avoid this problem, I suggest keeping on hand a couple of pairs of new, solid-colored socks that are still in the package. That way, you know the color and you know for sure that they match. If you are not sure what color to wear, black socks will go with almost any interview suit.

### Hair

Your hair should be short to medium in length, and well groomed. Unless you are interviewing for a creative position like software development or musician, hair down to your shoulders is not a wise idea. Definitely make sure you are clean-shaven. If you have facial hair, keep it trimmed and shaped properly.

### Hands

Hands are also very important in conveying a positive and successful image. Your fingernails should be trimmed and clean, or even manicured. I recommend that you limit the jewelry on your hands to a wedding ring if you are married and nothing if you are not.

### Jewelry

Other jewelry on men should be minimal. Avoid wearing necklaces, chains or bracelets. Watches are acceptable, as well as modest tie tacks, tie clips and cuff links. Do not wear an earring or a nose ring.

## Dress For Success—Women

### Business Suits

For women, professional attire also includes a business suit. In selecting the color, you need not limit yourself to solid gray or blue, but do not wear wild patterns. Try to stay away from long blazers. If you are wearing a suit with a skirt, keep the skirt at a conservative length. Short skirts do not convey a professional image and can detract from your positive message. For jackets that have a V-neck opening, be aware of how much skin is exposed. To minimize excessive skin exposure, a matching scarf or blouse is appropriate.

### Blouses

When considering what to wear with your suit, the blouse selection is very important. Your blouse should be a solid color or tasteful print, but should never be made of a transparent material. Blouses made of lace or chiffon should be avoided. These materials are more for a night out than the office. In any case, you should also wear a camisole under your blouse. Wearing a camisole will prevent any unsightly lines from showing through.

### Shoes and Hose

Make sure your shoes are professional and match the business attire. When it comes to hosiery, you should always wear a conservative color or a color that complements the suit. Conservative colors are nude, suntan, taupe or black. If you wear bright-colored hose, it can be distracting to interviewers and take away from your overall professional image. Unless you are interviewing for a nursing position, don't wear white hose.

### Accessories

In selecting a handbag or briefcase, choose one that complements your outfit, is small or medium sized, and made of leather. Large bags can be unsightly and create an appearance of disorganization.

### Hair

Hair is a very important component to your overall presentation. You should have very manageable hair, preferably no longer than shoulder length. If your hair is long, you should wear it up or in a manner that is perceived to be stylish and professional. You don't want to look like you just walked out of a beach house or a nightclub.

### Makeup

I recommend subtle and tasteful makeup. A bit of blush and lipstick should be worn at a minimum to accentuate your features. Depending on your complexion, natural colors like browns or tans may be best. For your lips, soft reds, corals and pinks are the best colors. Be careful though; too much makeup can be a detriment and a distraction.

### Hands

Your hands should also be well manicured. Fingernails should be painted either a conservative red, light pink, French style or with a clear polish.

### Jewelry

When it comes to jewelry, keep it simple. If you are engaged or married, feel free to wear those rings. However, try to avoid wearing other rings. I have seen women in interviews wear a ring on every finger. This does not convey a professional image. Plus, it is very difficult to give a good handshake when a person wears too many rings. When you shake a person's hand, you want to feel a firm grip. Jewelry inhibits that.

Earrings can also impact your overall appearance. Too many earrings or extremely large earrings draw attention away from your presentation and message.

Finally, do not wear religious jewelry. There is no need to bring religion into the interview. You want interviewers to focus on your skills and talent, not your faith.

The bottom-line is to dress for success—not to make a fashion statement.

You want to look professional and like a businessperson, not a nightclub patron. Dressing well is essential in creating a successful first impression.

## Dress For Success—Final Areas of Consideration
## For Both Men and Women

What if you walk into the interview all spiffed up, but the interviewer is wearing casual clothes?

If you are a man, you can take off your jacket and loosen your tie a bit. This will allow you to appear a bit more casual.

If you are a woman, you can focus on posture and nonverbal language. Try to appear casual. Personal appearances aside, there are other aspects that can impact your overall appearance.

### Freshen Your Breath

Having fresh breath is extremely important in making a good impression. If your breath smells like garlic, onions, cigarettes or even coffee, you might offend interviewers. Think about it. Do you feel comfortable when you are talking to a person with bad breath? Most likely you do not. So, prior to the interview, please be sure to brush your teeth, gargle with mouthwash and use a long-lasting breath freshener.

### Clean Your Car

What kind of car are you driving? Do you have a clean car? If not, clean it before the interview! Interviewers may want to walk you to your car. You want to leave them with a positive impression, not a negative one. Is your car presentable, or does it have more dents than a beer can that fell off a five-story building? If, your car is not presentable, then rent one or take public transportation.

### Press Your Suit

What about the condition of the clothes you are going to wear for the interview? Did you just press your suit? If not, get it pressed!

### Use Professional Writing Instruments

What about your note pad? Don't walk into the interview with a grade school yellow notepad. Get a professional note pad. And, don't forget about using a nice pen. A.T. Cross Company manufactures attractive and relatively inexpensive pens that present a very professional image. Don't walk into the interview with a ten-cent disposable pen. You will leave a bad impression.

### Leave Your Cell Phone in the Car

If you must keep your cell phone and beeper with you, then turn them off before you go into the interview. Nothing is more annoying than a cell phone or beeper ringing during the interview. It is distracting, ruins the flow, and if you (*GASP!*) take the call, you convey the impression that your call is more important than your interview. You can always return the call later.

# HAVE FUN

Ah, I almost forgot the most important aspect of all to a successful interview—FUN!

The interview is one of the most exciting aspects of job hunting. Enjoy it and have fun with the whole process.

You may be thinking, "Interviewing gives me headaches and sweaty palms! It's no fun!"

But interviewing is fun if you have the right approach and the right attitude. Interviewing is nothing more than a game. There are winners and losers. In order for you to be the winner, you have to have a better strategy than the loser's line of attack.

## Talent Alone Does Not Win!

Talent is not everything. Often, the sports teams that recruit and possess the best players still don't win. Just look at the NCAA basketball tournament. Every year there seems to be at least one team from a small school that reaches the final four. On paper, they look like just an average team. The reason they make it that far is that they put no pressure on themselves to win. They have a better strategy and they go out and have fun. Thus, being more relaxed and confident, they make more shots, foul less and make fewer mistakes. The end result is they win.

Have you ever noticed that the people who have the most fun on their jobs tend to be the most successful people in their profession? Interviewing is the same. You have to have fun.

## Treat Interviewing like a Game!

Treat interviewing and job hunting like a game. Why not see how many offers you can get? Why not try to anticipate questions before they are asked? I used to have fun by trying to guess how the people would look just by their name. By taking an attitude that interviewing is like a game, you will be much more relaxed and confident.

Laugh at your learning experiences. The more fun you have, the better you will perform.

After all, interviewing is a game for interviewers as well. They may have fun by seeing how you handle a tough question or how you stack up against the others. In fact, some of my counterparts ask some crazy questions just to make the process more fun and to make the interviewee squirm. One of my friends, a fellow manager at a company I worked for, asks the question, "Why are manhole covers round?"

In asking this question, he looks for how candidates handle a completely unrelated and utterly useless question. He also looks to see how someone handles a situation where they did not know the answer. He bonged many candidates because they stumbled and tried to make up an answer even though they clearly had no idea why. This question tells a lot about a person's morals. If someone makes up an answer to this question in the interview, what would they do in front of a customer?

## Be Honest!

If you are ever asked a question where you do not know the answer, be honest and say you don't know. Say that you would be more than happy to research the answer and get back to them. Lying and making up answers to questions is the surest way to be rejected.

## So, Why Are Manhole Covers Round?

The answer is that a circular shaped lid, unlike a square or an oval, won't fall through the opening. There's no way to position a round cover to slip through a slightly smaller hole of the same shape. That's because a circle has a constant width (the same width all the way around).

However, an oval has a shape that is longer than it is wide. Thus, you can always find a way to slip an oval lid through a hole of the same shape. That's also true of a square or a six-sided, hexagonal cover. If you try to cut those shapes out of a piece of paper, you will see that you can slip the cut out piece right through the opening created by it.

My favorite question to ask, as I interviewed candidates was, "Why should I recommend you to be hired over the other people I have interviewed?" I couldn't wait to ask that question, because it was amazing how differently people answered it.

You can win if you relax and do not put pressure on yourself. Look at every interview as an opportunity for you to sell yourself, an opportunity to learn and an opportunity to have some FUN. Remember, if you get the cane around the neck, so what? You will have gained knowledge from the experience and be that much closer to your dream job.

## Try Rewarding Yourself

Another tactic that a friend used, to make interviewing fun, was for her to treat herself to something nice after each interview—regardless of how it went. That way she always looked forward to the interview. Maybe you want to reward yourself with a nice lunch or a massage. Whether you choose to reward yourself after each interview, or to treat each interview like a game, you can have fun with the entire process.

## Look at Interviewing in Two Ways

First, you have to *sell* yourself. Second, *make the company sell itself to you*. You have a lot of talent and positive qualities. Good employees are not easy to find. There are a lot of mediocre people out there. Don't sell yourself short. You have a tremendous amount to offer and you should be proud of yourself. If an interviewer cannot express why you should work at his or her company, then maybe that company is not worth joining.

To win, be relaxed, confident, have a well-thought-out strategy and most of all, have FUN!

## THE 6 PHASES OF A SUCCESSFUL JOB INTERVIEW

For any interview to be successful, you must cover all of the following phases: Introduction, Rapport Building, Interest Generation, Qualification, Strengths Review and The Close.

---

### The 6 Phases of a Successful Job Interview

1) Introduction

2) Rapport Building

3) Interest Generation

4) Qualification

5) Strengths Review

6) The Close

---

## 1) INTRODUCTION

The first step to any interview is the introduction. This is where that important first impression is made. It is during the introduction that interviewers see how you are dressed, how you shake their hand, and the presence you command when you enter a room.

During the introduction, you want to create a terrific first impression. You want to plan in advance how you are going to introduce yourself. I used to write down a script that I practiced time and time again. Of course, I would not bring that script in with me, but I always wanted to be prepared.

**Example:**

"Good morning, my name is \_\_\_\_\_ _____, currently of _____company. I greatly appreciate you giving me the opportunity to meet with you today."

You will typically introduce yourself while shaking hands. This is a good time to discuss some basic handshake guidelines.

## Handshake Guidelines

The handshake is usually one of the first events in an interview. If you are a woman interviewing with a man, be the first to offer your hand in a handshake. If you are a woman interviewing with another woman, let her be the first to offer you a handshake.

If you are a man interviewing with another man, it is all right to lead with your hand in a handshake. However, if you are a man interviewing with a woman, always let her be the first to offer her hand.

Whether you are male or female, make sure you give a firm shake. Do not squeeze the person's hand as if you are ringing water out of a wet sock, but be firm enough so that the other person doesn't feel like he or she is shaking a dead fish. A good handshake shows a sign of confidence and respect. A sweaty, weak and flimsy handshake says that you lack self-esteem and you don't think you're the right person for the job.

## What If Your Hands are Clammy?

If you can't control your sweaty palms, right before the interview wash your hands in warm water and soap, and dry them off completely. The soap will dry out your hands and what the soap did not dry, the towel will. Plus, you will be clean and confident.

## After the Handshake

After the handshake, the interviewer likely will ask you to sit down. At this time, a good idea is to take out an extra copy of your resume and hand it to the interviewer.

**Example:**

"I have brought an extra copy of my resume for your convenience."

By providing your name and a copy of your resume, interviewers will remember you. The introduction step is usually the briefest step of the interview process, but is one of the most important because first impressions are always the most vivid. The interviewer will likely be meeting with several people, so you want to stand out and be remembered positively.

# 2) RAPPORT BUILDING

The second phase of the interview, and one that continues throughout the remainder of the interview, is rapport building. Developing good rapport is critical to a successful interview. People tend to like those who remind them of themselves. You surround yourself with friends. You feel comfortable with friends who have qualities and characteristics similar to yours. In establishing a positive rapport with interviewers, you want them to consciously and subconsciously feel comfortable with you (almost like a friend) and believe that you have similar characteristics.

This is done both verbally and non-verbally.

## Verbal Communication

All interviewers have their own unique styles of verbal communication. Style encompasses tone of voice, pitch, rate and volume. One's voice can show a person's emotions and personality. Some may come across as pleasant and friendly, while others may be very serious and cold. You do not want to mimic interviewers, but you do want to speak in a similar manner.

### Tone

For instance, say the interviewer has a very friendly tone and is extremely cheerful. Do not try to be overwhelmingly businesslike and monotone. You will fail miserably. Instead, try to also be cheerful and enthusiastic. On the other hand, if the interviewer is intensely businesslike and shows little emotion, your dialogue should respect that style. If you try to be overly cheerful to a person who is not as light-hearted in nature, you will not succeed.

### Pitch, Rate and Volume

Also, it is very important to notice the pitch, rate and volume of voice. If some interviewers speak in a low pitch, very slowly and softly, and you talk in a rapid, loud manner, you will overwhelm them.

### Word Selection

Additionally, you want to use words that are similar in conversation to those of the interviewer. If the interviewer uses emotional words like feel, love, beautiful, etc., then you want to incorporate some of those words into your conversation. Conversely, if the interviewer uses more factual based words in conversation like created, developed, structured, etc., then you want to make sure you use phrases that are similar.

People enjoy working with individuals who make them feel comfortable and who are like themselves. You can use verbal communication to your advantage by talking in a fashion that matches your interviewers. If interviewers see some of their qualities in you, they will be much more receptive to what you have to say.

### Nonverbal Communication

90 percent of face-to-face communication is nonverbal. As a result, in many respects, nonverbal communication is more important than verbal communication. Nonverbal communication includes appearance, facial expressions, posture, eye contact, gestures and scent.

You can interpret nonverbal gestures to understand the true feelings of interviewers and use nonverbal communication to build positive rapport and to make a point.

## Facial Expressions

First, let's consider facial expressions.

Is the interviewer smiling and nodding in agreement to what you are saying?

**If yes:**

Keep going—you are doing great.

**If no:**

If you see interviewers with blank expressions on their faces, or almost nodding off, then something is wrong. In this case, let the interviewers do more of the talking. Make your answers shorter and ask more questions.

Suppose the interviewer has a very serious face, as if it belonged on Mt. Rushmore. In this case, be serious. If your facial expression is all smiles and you look like Howdy Doody, then you will agitate the interviewer.

On the other hand, if the interviewer positively beams, then smile and be friendly.

## Posture

Posture can also help you determine how the interview is progressing. If the interviewer is sitting in an open position and slightly reclined, this demonstrates a certain level of comfort or a general agreement with what you are saying. In this case, you should also sit in an open position and slightly reclined. Do not mimic; be discreet.

If the interviewer is sitting up straight and forward, do not sit in the chair like an oversized ball of putty. Position yourself like the interviewer. Otherwise, you will convey the attitude that you could not care less how the interview turns out.

If the interviewer is sitting with arms crossed and straight as an arrow, then probably you are not doing too well. However, if the interviewer leans forward with the classic hand-on-the-chin pose then you really hit a hot button. Continue emphasizing whatever you said that interested the interviewer.

## What should you do when interviewers have their arms crossed?

Either you need to change what you are saying or you need to do something to get that person to relax. A trick I learned years ago is that you also should sit with your arms crossed.

Then, slowly drop one arm and then the other. Often, interviewers will follow you and drop their arms as well. If not, then you are in trouble and you need to understand where you are going wrong. Ask if you are focusing on the information that the interviewer wants to discuss.

### Example #1:

"There is so much great information I could tell you, what would you like me to focus on first?" (Answering a vague question where you could easily ramble on)

### Example #2:

"Where would you like me to start?" (After being asked about yourself or your job history)

## Eye Contact

Perhaps the most telling nonverbal cue is eye contact. If interviewers look you straight in the eye while listening to you, then you are communicating. If the interviewers are looking at the stuffed fish on the wall or the bubbles in the water cooler, then they are not hearing a word you are saying. You want to make sure you establish good eye contact with the interviewer. Eye contact shows that you mean what you say.

## Gestures

You can also use nonverbal gestures to punctuate what you are saying. By smiling when you say something positive about yourself, or by being serious when you mention your work experience, you can emphasize your point. You can also lean forward or raise your hand to emphasize a particular strength or area of importance.

You see, not only is nonverbal communication significant in understanding the interviewer and building rapport, it is critical in emphasizing the message you're trying to get across.

To enhance your nonverbal communication skills, look for nonverbal communication in your everyday life and practice it. Whether you are talking to a friend or meeting with a business associate, consciously look for nonverbal clues. The more you practice the better you will be able to use nonverbal communication and gestures in your interview.

## Scent

Believe it or not, you also need to be aware of the cologne or perfume that you wear. Wear just enough to create a light scent. Do not bathe in the bottle, it can be offensive. Some people have perfume allergies and you don't want interviewers to have an allergic reaction to you. So be subtle in your scent, or forego it completely.

However, don't forget to wear antiperspirant or deodorant. If you smell like the inside of a gym locker, you will turn people off. If you're one who sweats, make sure you wear light clothes and a jacket or blazer that covers up your sweat.

### Rapport is Developed on a Subconscious Level

The tips I have given you will ensure you give the interviewer's subconscious mind a positive impression. This is done by subtly employing the verbal and nonverbal communication style of the interviewer. The more similar you appear to the subconscious mind of the interviewer, the greater the chance you will have of succeeding in the interview.

## 3) INTEREST GENERATION

The next phase of the interview is generating interest. While building rapport is extremely important, you must be able to generate interest in yourself to succeed in the interview. This is where the interviewer will decide whether or not to listen to you. Here, you want to communicate what you can do for the company and person interviewing you.

To generate interest, you want to express enthusiasm and excitement. You also need some nugget of information that will excite the interviewer. This can be difficult because before you can generate interest, you need to know what interests the interviewer.

In the preparation phase, you identified key industry phrases and challenges. Before the interview, revisit these items and develop a couple of simple sentences that convey an interesting fact about you that could intrigue in the interviewer.

**Example:**

"I am excited about this opportunity . . . In my current position I have successfully reduced expenses by over 35 percent and increased productivity by over 20 percent . . . This is a great opportunity to leverage my experience and become an immediate asset to your company."

Another great way to generate interest, if the flow of the interview allows you to do this, is to ask the interviewer a question.

**Example:**

"If you had your ideal candidate for this position, what qualities and characteristics would be important to you?"

The interviewer might mention characteristics such as motivated, team player, good communications skills and willingness to learn.

### Focus on a Couple of Hot Buttons

Now that you have an idea of what your interviewer is looking for, you can focus on one or two key areas to generate interest.

**Example:**

"That's great. Throughout my career, I have consistently demonstrated that I am a very motivated person."

Immediately, you can generate interest. If you don't ask interviewers what is important, you may talk about attributes that they don't care about.

## 4) QUALIFICATION

The next phase of the interview is where both you and the interviewers see if there is a mutual fit. Remember all of those questions you prepared for and answered earlier in this book? Now is the time you will put all that hard work to use.

In this phase, both you and the interviewers ask questions to qualify each other. If in the Generate Interest phase you were not able to ask the question, "If you had your ideal candidate for this position, what qualities and characteristics would be important to you?" then you must figure out a way at the beginning of the Qualification phase to ask it.

### Some additional questions that you could ask during this phase include:

"What is it about your company that you enjoy the most?"

"Does your company have high or low employee turnover?"

"What are the key attributes that makes your company better than others in the industry?"

"How do you reward top performers?"

"If I exceed expectations, what is the typical timeframe to get a raise?"

"Do you have any additional questions?"

"What is the next step in this interview process?"

"When do you expect to make a decision on this position?"

"How quickly could I start if I was accepted for this position?"

### Your Questions Should Be Assumptive

Do you see the tone of the previous questions? They are all positive and assumptive questions. Each one fosters valuable feedback and, more importantly, will impress the person interviewing you. By asking these types of questions, you display a confidence that says, "I know I am the right person for this job. Why look further?"

I am not recommending that you ask all of the previous questions, but you should ask a couple. You have the right to know the answers. Otherwise, how will you know if the position interests you? Also, by asking intelligent, assumptive questions, you demonstrate confidence. Interviewers can sense this confidence and will be more than happy to answer your questions.

### Ask Questions at the Appropriate Time

Don't just fire one question after another at interviewers, especially at the beginning. Usually interviewers will ask you at the end of this phase if you have any questions. That is the best time to ask them.

## 5) STRENGTHS REVIEW

This is where you recap the strengths that you covered in the interview. Here, restate what interviewers say they are looking for in their ideal candidates.

**Example:**

"To summarize what we have discussed, you are looking for a person who is a leader and one that needs little supervision. Is that correct?" (Pause . . . hopefully there will be a nod in agreement.) "That's great because I thrive in entrepreneurial environments . . . especially when it requires the necessity to think on my feet."

Be sure to ask at some point during your strengths review if there is any additional information that the interviewer would like to discuss.

## 6) THE CLOSE

This is the best part of the interview. This is where you determine whether or not you have a good chance of getting the job. This is where you go for the sale—a job offer! In going for the close, be confident and excited. Summarize your skills and relate how your expertise will benefit the interviewer and the company.

**Example:**

"I want to thank you for giving me the opportunity to meet with you. This job sounds exciting and I feel I could really help your company reduce costs and streamline processes. I am looking forward to talking with you in the future. When can I expect to hear back from you?"

Often, when interviewers like you, they are as excited as you are. When interviewers find the right person, they show enthusiasm and give you a specific timeframes on when they will follow up. It is not a positive sign when interviewers are inconclusive and vague. Try to pin them down to a specific timeframe.

**Example:**

"What is the next step in the decision-making process?"

During the close of the interview, remain positive, self-assured and enthusiastic. As we have discussed before, if you do not exemplify these traits, you will just be another mediocre candidate. Give interviewers a reason to want to hire you. Act like a winner and interviewers will perceive you as one!

# HOW TO HAVE A SUCCESSFUL JOB INTERVIEW

## CHECKLIST SUMMARY

✔ **KEEP your SPIRITS HIGH**

✔ **Make the INTERVIEWER FEEL GOOD**

✔ **Remember . . . YOU ARE EQUAL**

✔ **DRESS for SUCCESS**

✔ **Leave your CELL PHONE in the CAR**

✔ **PRACTICE the 6 PHASES of a SUCCESSFUL JOB INTERVIEW**

✔ **Create scripts for the INTRODUCTION and GENERATE INTEREST PHASES**

✔ **Look for NONVERBAL COMMUNICATION in your everyday LIFE**

✔ **Treat INTERVIEWING like a GAME and HAVE FUN**

✔ **REWARD yourself after each INTERVIEW**

**"Talent alone does not WIN!"**

# SECRET #10

## DON'T JUST TALK ABOUT IT . . . DO IT!

- **Take Immediate Action**
- **Treat Job Hunting Like a Job**
- **Jump In . . . The Water's Fine**

Congratulations. You now have the foundation you need to be successful in your job hunt. You have learned everything from developing a positive attitude to selling yourself in the interview.

Hopefully, this has been a fun and rewarding experience for you. I know I have enjoyed sharing my knowledge with you. These secrets, tips and techniques will undoubtedly help you achieve success.

However, there is one secret that I have yet to mention. Most unfortunately, without this secret, you can not succeed in your job hunt—Take Immediate Action!

## TAKE IMMEDIATE ACTION!

You must take the knowledge you have gained from this book and take immediate action. I can't tell you how many people I have seen who just sat on their duffs waiting for a job to drop in their lap. Then they wonder why they can't find a job.

I know the concept of taking action is not easy. Change is always scary. But without action, you cannot succeed. Sometimes it is easier to start by taking baby steps. What I have found helpful is to put together a daily "To Do" list. On this list, I put items like "Research 10 companies" or "Make 5 phone calls." When you write out step-by-step what you have to do, it makes things much easier.

## TREAT JOB HUNTING LIKE A JOB!

Getting a new job is a job in itself. Anyone who tells you otherwise is mistaken. If you were working at a full-time or part-time job, you would not blow off the job days at a time or show up late, would you? No, you would go to work every day and consistently show up on time.

Hunting for a job requires the same effort. You must dedicate a certain amount of time devoted solely to the purpose of the job hunt.

*If you are unemployed,* you should dedicate eight hours a day to job hunting activities. This can be spent in a variety of ways from doing research, to networking, to improving your resume. Practice counts as well. If you have an interview coming up, practice as much as possible. Remember the best athletes, they perform at their peaks because they practice every day. Just ask Tiger Woods or Shaquille O'Neal. Why should you settle for less?

*If you are employed or a student,* you should devote at least two to three hours a day. If you can not afford to do that, then schedule two or three days out of the week to where you can spend two to three hours at a time focused on job hunting. In this case, treat job hunting like a part-time job.

I know this sounds tough, and I know you may be intimidated by what I am saying. But if you don't take job hunting seriously, you will not get the job you want, in the time you want.

## JUMP IN . . . THE WATER'S FINE!

I am sure you have gone into a swimming pool or hot tub before. Have you ever stepped in and felt the pool was too cold or the tub too hot. I know I have. Every time I went into a pool or tub one foot at a time, it was always difficult. I always found that it was much easier to just jump in. The first couple of seconds are always tough, but the body adjusts quickly.

Beginning your job hunt is the same as jumping into a pool. If you start too slowly, or not at all, you will never get into the job hunt and you will prolong your misery. But, if you jump into the job hunt with both feet, you will realize it is not so bad. So, just jump in and you'll do fine.

Like a locomotive, it takes time to pick up speed. Once you build momentum, you can't help but succeed. The faster you start, the more momentum you will pick up. The more momentum you pick up, the greater your chances will be of getting the job you have always wanted.

Hopefully by now, you have completed the exercises in this book and you are ready to begin your job hunt. If not, complete the exercises as soon as possible and then start implementing the secrets.

## Now it is Up to You!

I've given you the foundation necessary to succeed in your job hunting efforts.

*If you are employed*, you can either stay in a job you are not happy with or you can take action and live out your dreams.

*If you are unemployed,* you can either stay unemployed or you can go out there, start selling yourself and bust your hump to get the job you want.

*If you are a student,* you can remain a permanent student and not deal with reality or you can get excited, jump in and get that job.

I can't make the ultimate decision for you. Only you can make your own decisions.

## YOU ARE GREAT!

I know you are a fantastic person with awesome credentials. You are the type person that any company would want to hire. It is my hope and sincere desire that you go out there and get the job you want.

My purpose in writing this book is simple. I want to help as many people as possible improve their lives by getting the jobs they want, as quickly as possible. If I have helped motivate you to go find the job you want, then I have partially achieved my objectives. However, my ultimate goal is for you to go out there and actually get that job of your dreams.

## So Go Out There and Do It!

Jump in and, most importantly, have fun. Life is too short to get stressed over job hunting. If you follow what is discussed in this book you will succeed. So relax, take action, and be proud of who you are. I am proud of you for taking the courage and the time to read this book.

# DON'T JUST TALK ABOUT IT . . . DO IT!

## CHECKLIST SUMMARY

✔ Take IMMEDIATE ACTION!

✔ Put together a DAILY "TO DO" LIST

✔ TREAT the JOB HUNT like a JOB!

✔ Make at least 5 PHONE CALLS per DAY

✔ Jump in, the water's FINE!

✔ Only YOU can DETERMINE your ULTIMATE SUCCESS

**"Once you build momentum, you can't help but succeed."**

# 7 BONUS SECRETS

Ah, one of the best things to strive for in life is to try to exceed the expectations of others. I am having so much fun working with you, I want to exceed your expectations and provide you with some bonus secrets that will be helpful in your job hunt.

- SELL YOURSELF AFTER THE INTERVIEW
- HOW TO ACCEPT A JOB OFFER
- HOW TO REJECT A JOB OFFER
- HOW TO NEGOTIATE A BETTER JOB OFFER
- THE BEST TIMES TO INTERVIEW
- THE PROPER INTERVIEWING ETIQUETTE
- THE LEGALITIES OF INTERVIEWING

**"Always strive to exceed the expectations of others and you will prosper!"**

# BONUS #i

## SELL YOURSELF AFTER THE INTERVIEW

- **Summarize the Interview**
- **Follow Up**
- **Do the Small Things**

**P**hew! The interview is over—or is it?

## SUMMARIZE THE INTERVIEW

Just because the interview is over doesn't mean your work is finished. After each interview, write down a few notes on what was discussed during the interview.

First, make sure you have the correct spelling of the names of all the people you met. Ideally, you asked each person for a business card. Then, write down key points you discussed. This will help you prepare for future interviews and also help you determine if you are interested in the position.

Often, I have been saved by the fact that I took notes after an interview. When talking with several companies, you'd be surprised at how hard it is to remember what has been said. In subsequent interviews, you may want to refer back to what others have mentioned.

**Example:**

"In speaking with your head of sales, I learned that your company is very service oriented. How do you maintain this image?"

By writing down notes immediately after the interview, the information you received will still be fresh in your mind. This information will be helpful when you compare one position to another. One company may have better benefits, while another may have a position that is more interesting. By having good notes, you can accurately determine which job is best for you.

## Rate Your Performance

Also, when summarizing the interview, don't forget to rate your performance during the interview. Summarize the areas where you think you did well and also note the areas where you need to improve. This will help you learn from each interviewing experience. You can then focus on the areas you need to improve on in your future practicing sessions. When you summarize each interview, there is no such thing as a bad interview, because you can learn from the experience. *The only way you can fail on an interview is if you don't take the time to learn from it.*

# FOLLOW UP

After each interview, you should immediately type a thank you note to each person that you met. If you have good handwriting, a handwritten note on good stationary can also be an excellent touch. Even send the receptionist or secretary a thank you. You might be surprised to discover how much power a receptionist or secretary can have in an organization. They can either help or destroy your chances of getting a job.

Once you have typed up your letters, fax, e-mail or send them via priority overnight service.

## Why Go to This Time and Expense?

Well, if you want the job, then you need to do what it takes to get it. I can guarantee you that if an interviewer is on the fence and is not quite sure which person to choose, a simple thank you can make all the difference. If you send a fax, e-mail or overnight package, that person is going to say, "Wow! That's the kind of person I want to hire!"

I remember a time when I was really torn between two people I interviewed for a West Coast sales position. Both people did a great job interviewing. Both were polished and had excellent experience. Actually, I tried to convince the company to allow me to hire both of them. Unfortunately, they said no.

The first applicant I interviewed e-mailed me immediately upon her return to California. In the e-mail, she told me how excited she was about the opportunity and how successful she would be in the position. The second candidate I interviewed took two days to thank me via e-mail. Well, as you might imagine, I ended up hiring the first person due to the simple fact that she thanked me in a more timely fashion.

## DO THE SMALL THINGS

In interviewing, as well as in life, it is sometimes the smallest things that can make the biggest differences. By doing the little things like saying thank you via e-mail, you can make a difference. What's the worst that could happen? The worst that could happen is that you wasted a few minutes or hours of your time and a couple of dollars of your money. At least you will be at peace with yourself knowing you did everything you could to get the job. The most frustrating thing is failing at something because you did not give it your best shot. So what if it takes a couple of extra hours or you spend a couple of additional dollars? In the grand scheme of things, what's the big deal?

# SELL YOURSELF AFTER THE INTERVIEW

## CHECKLIST SUMMARY

✔ Take Notes and SUMMARIZE the INTERVIEW

✔ Ask yourself what you did WELL on in the interview and how you can IMPROVE for your NEXT INTERVIEW

✔ Send THANK YOU NOTES IMMEDIATELY . . . *IF NOT SOONER*

✔ Do the SMALL things that make a BIG DIFFERENCE

**"The most frustrating thing is failing at something because you did not give it your best shot!"**

# BONUS #ii

## HOW TO ACCEPT A JOB OFFER

- **Ask Questions**
- **Make the Call**
- **Show Excitement**

**G**etting a job offer is the ultimate prize in job interviewing. However, after the initial celebration you have to decide if you want to accept the offer. Whether you are accepting or rejecting an offer, the key is to contain your emotions. By remaining calm, you will make the right career decision.

### Questions:

**1) Is this a position I really want?**

**2) Are they offering me enough money?**

**3) Is this a short-term position or one with a good career path?**

**4) Will my personality match well with this company?**

**5) In three years, will I still want to work for this company?**

**6) Do I want to work for this type of boss?**

**7) Is the position in alignment with my ideal job mission statement and my values?**

## ASK QUESTIONS

Before making a decision, ask yourself a few questions about the job.

If after answering your questions, you want to accept the job, then do so enthusiastically!

## MAKE THE CALL

Call interviewers in a timely fashion. There is no reason to wait too long. Reply in a time-frame that is long enough to show that you are not desperate, but short enough to demonstrate your excitement for the job. I recommend thanking the person for the offer and saying that you will get back within a day or two with a final decision. You want to convey an image that you are in demand. However, it is perfectly acceptable, if you are happy with the offer, to accept it immediately. Only you will be able to judge the situation and do what is right.

In either case, limit your conversation; you do not want to "buy back the sale." Often, salespeople make the mistake of talking too much and actually losing or "buying back" the sale. Don't make this same mistake.

## SHOW EXCITEMENT

When you do decide to accept, do so in an excited tone. Accept the position and restate your enthusiasm. Then ask what the next step should be, and when and where you should report to work. Most importantly, thank interviewers for offering you a job and tell them that they made a great decision!

### Example:

"Good Morning Mr. _____ this is _____. I want to thank you so much for the job offer and I am calling you to accept. (Be enthusiastic!) You made a great decision and I know you will be thrilled with my efforts. What is the next step in the process? (Pause!) Again, thank you so much for giving me this opportunity. Have a great day!"

# HOW TO ACCEPT A JOB OFFER

## CHECKLIST SUMMARY

✔ **MAINTAIN your COMPOSURE**

✔ **ASK yourself some BASIC QUESTIONS**

✔ **MAKE SURE the JOB is RIGHT for YOU and that it is the JOB YOU WANT**

✔ **Make the CALL**

✔ **ACCEPT ENTHUSIASTICALLY**

✔ **SHOW EXCITEMENT**

✔ **Limit Your Conversation . . . DON'T "BUY BACK the SALE"**

**"Thank interviewers for offering you a job and tell them that they made a great decision!"**

# BONUS #iii

## HOW TO REJECT A JOB OFFER

- **Make Sure**
- **Respond Quickly**
- **Keep Your Options Open**

## MAKE SURE YOU ARE MAKING THE RIGHT DECISION!

The job hunt can be a very emotional journey. Various emotions can cause you to make rash decisions. Before you decide to formally reject the offer, make sure the position fails to match your criteria. In the last chapter, I covered seven questions you should ask yourself before accepting a job. You should ask these same questions before rejecting a job.

The key is to take your emotions out of the decision and look at the situation objectively. If after doing so you are not comfortable with the situation then reject the job. If you are not sure, ask some of your friends and family what they would do.

## RESPOND QUICKLY AND COURTEOUSLY

If you want to reject the offer, then make sure you do so quickly. Give interviewers a chance to look elsewhere; you never want to burn any bridges. A phone call or a letter is appropriate. Make sure you thank the interviewers for their time. Also, flatter the interviewers. Say it was a tough decision, but it was not the ideal fit at this time.

## KEEP YOUR OPTIONS OPEN

Mention that you are very impressed with the company and that you would like to keep your options open if a better fit opens up in the future. You never know when in the future you might want to work for the company. Try to be as complimentary as possible towards the person and the company and part on gracious terms.

**Example:**

"Good afternoon Ms. _____ this is _____. I want to thank you so much for the job offer. Unfortunately at this time I have to decline. I am extremely impressed with both you and your company. This is a very difficult decision. The offer just isn't the right fit at this time. I greatly appreciate the time you spent with me and I'd like to keep the dialogue open for the future. Again, thank you so much for your time."

# HOW TO REJECT A JOB OFFER

## CHECKLIST SUMMARY

---

✔ Maintain your COMPOSURE

✔ Make Sure You Are Making the RIGHT DECISION

✔ RESPOND QUICKLY

✔ Reject GRACIOUSLY

✔ Keep your OPTIONS OPEN

---

## "You never want to burn any bridges!"

## HOW TO NEGOTIATE
## A BETTER JOB OFFER

● 7 Building Blocks of a Successful Negotiation

**W**hat if you really like the company and the job, but you are disappointed in the salary offered? This is really a touchy subject. First, look at all of the accompanying perks. If, you still feel the offer is short of your expectations, then be honest.

This is a difficult topic, because in any negotiation, you can lose. In this case you can lose the job. However, if you are not going to be happy working for what they proposed, then you have no other alternative than to negotiate.

To successfully negotiate you need to follow seven fundamental steps.

---

**7 Building Blocks of a Successful Negotiation**

1) **Research the Market**

2) **Exhibit Confidence**

3) **Create Demand**

4) **Demonstrate Excitement**

5) **Find a Win-Win**

6) **Be Honest**

7) **Expand the Playing Field**

---

## 1) RESEARCH THE MARKET

Before entering into any job negotiation, research the market to see how your job offer compares with others. Look at the title of the position you are being offered. For instance, a director will typically get paid more than a manager will. See what comparable titles earn in your targeted industry. In doing research, you will have an idea of how your offer compares with others and you will have an indication of how much negotiating room you have.

## 2) EXHIBIT CONFIDENCE

When negotiating with interviewers, you need to maintain your confidence. Any weakness here will cause interviewers to not budge on the offer. They may even yank the offer off the table all together. If you come across as confident and willing to lose the job if necessary, you are more likely to get a better offer. After all, out of all the people they interviewed, these companies chose you! That means they want you. Be confident!

However, being confident does not mean being demanding. People don't like to be told what they have to do. Have balance in your approach. Be firm, not demanding!

**Example:**

"I know I will be a tremendous asset to your company and I appreciate your offer . . . However, I must tell you that I was expecting a salary of about $10,000 more. The position is awesome and your company is fantastic, but, unfortunately, I can't accept the job under these terms . . . I would very much like to work for you and your company. Is there any way we can meet somewhere in between?"

## 3) CREATE DEMAND

In any negotiation, when one party is in demand or has more control of a situation, typically the other party realizes they need to be flexible. Think about dating. Right or wrong, many people feel that if their significant other is also seeing other people, they need to be more generous and considerate towards that person. In other words, couples are usually more flexible with each other when they are not exclusive.

Negotiating for a job is much the same. You want to show an image that many companies are looking to hire you and that your skills are in demand. You want to convey the message, that, there are other potential offers out there.

**Example:**

"I am looking at several companies and I am the most excited about your position . . . However, the numbers you offered are less than what I believe I am worth."

## 4) DEMONSTRATE EXCITEMENT

As you can see in the prior two steps, it is critical to show excitement for the job at hand. If you do not appear enthusiastic about the job, then they will not sweeten your offer. If, on the other hand, you are excited and confident, and they are just a few dollars short, then you will have a better chance of getting a sweetened offer.

## 5) FIND A WIN-WIN

For any negotiation to be successful, the end result has to be a win-win situation. That means both sides have to feel like they are better off as a result of the negotiation. Many companies will purposely leave a little room for negotiation. The key here is to show how the company will benefit by giving you more money.

You also need to demonstrate that you are willing to give as well.

**Example:**

"As I mentioned earlier, the offer is about $10,000 short of my expectations . . . I know with my tremendous enthusiasm, experience and proven track record, I will more than make up for that difference . . . However, to show my willingness to come to work for you, if we can meet somewhere in the middle, I can enthusiastically accept your position."

The key here is to use a figure that is higher than what you are actually looking for so that you can meet in the middle. For instance, if the offer was $5,000 less than you had hoped for, then say it was $10,000 less and ask to meet in the middle. If the offer was $10,000 less, then say it was $15,000 - $20,000 less than your expectations.

The same technique can be used on vacation time and other aspects of the offer. If the company wants you bad enough, they will be willing to negotiate. Just realize your limits and don't push for too much.

## 6) BE HONEST

If your mother was like mine, she always said, "Honesty is the best policy." This is true for negotiations as well. If the offer is for less money than you had hoped, you should be honest that you want more money. If the vacation time is not enough, you need to tell them that.

However, some things in the negotiating process kind of push honesty to the limit. As I mentioned earlier, you want to convey an image that you are in demand, and you want to quote a figure that is higher than what you are willing to accept. Is that dishonest?

Well, depending how you say things, you can be honest or dishonest. I suggest you speak the truth. Notice, for instance, that in creating a demand, I did not mention that you have job offers from other companies. Instead, I said that you "were looking at companies that may be offering more money." If you are trying to get interviews at other companies, then this is true.

In asking for more money, you would love to get $10,000 more instead of $5,000, wouldn't you? Of course you would! You are just willing to settle for less.

I know some of this may seem like I am stretching honesty a bit. My basic point, though, is to make sure you do not lie. If you don't have offers from other companies, then don't say you do. If you don't feel you are worth $10,000, more then don't say so. Ultimately, you will be the judge on what you can and can't say. The point is if you are honest throughout the process you will be more confident and have a greater chance of getting a better offer.

## 7) EXPAND THE PLAYING FIELD

The final aspect of negotiating is to expand the scope of the negotiation. For instance, let's say the company offered you $10,000 less than your expectation. Would you accept the offer if they doubled the number of stock options or if they granted you an extra week of vacation? Sometimes, companies may have flexibility in one area but not in another.

So be creative. There are many ways to come to a resolution that makes both sides happy. Figure out what you are willing to accept and to go for it. Just be aware that the company always reserves the right to refuse negotiation and may tell you to take it or leave it. If you have been honest with yourself and the company throughout the process, yet the offer is still unacceptable and the company will not improve it, then I would reject the offer. You want to be happy, and compensation is an important factor in job satisfaction.

### If a Company Doesn't Want to Negotiate—You Don't Want to Work There

Often, if a company is not willing to negotiate, then it is not a very flexible organization and probably not one you want to work for anyway. Only you will be able to decide what is right. Negotiation can bring you a better offer . . . but it can also cause you to lose your offer. Weigh all of the risks and potential rewards before you enter into any negotiating process.

# HOW TO NEGOTIATE FOR A BETTER JOB OFFER

## CHECKLIST SUMMARY

✔ **Maintain your COMPOSURE**

✔ **Ask yourself some basic QUESTIONS**

✔ **MAKE SURE the JOB is RIGHT for YOU and that it is the JOB YOU WANT**

✔ **Research the OFFER to determine its COMPETITIVENESS**

✔ **Propose a WIN-WIN SOLUTION**

✔ **MAINTAIN your CONFIDENCE . . . after all, they WANT YOU**

**"Weigh all of the risks and potential rewards before you enter into any negotiating process."**

# BONUS #v

## THE BEST TIMES TO INTERVIEW

- **First is Best**
- **Tuesday or Thursday**
- **9:30 am - 10:30 am**

Most companies will interview more than one person for a given position. Besides having read this book, how can you gain the advantage when competing against others? One way is if you have a choice of when to interview. During job fairs and on-campus interviewing, often you can choose when to interview. Like a horse race, your "post" position, for the interview, can determine your chances of success.

How does timing affect your opportunity? If you are the fifth person to interview, and the third person made an incredible impression, you lose. The precedent will have been set and the interviewer will have already determined that the third person is the one for the job.

## FIRST IS BEST

You should always try to be the first person to interview. By being first, you can set the expectation level. Everyone will have to measure up to you. Also, like first impressions, the interviewer will remember the most about the person who interviewed first. If you have an outstanding interview, it will be tough for anyone after you to succeed.

The last time I interviewed people, I was hiring for a sales position. The first person I interviewed was fantastic. It was like I was interviewing myself in a mirror. This guy answered every question the way I would have, had I been on the other side of the desk. Once that interview was over, I knew those who followed were going to have a tough time. Sure enough, only one, of the remaining eight, came close enough to be invited back for a second interview.

### What If You Can't Interview First?

Don't despair if you do not have control over the time of the interview. If you are not the first person to interview, the key is to raise the bar to make you stand out. You can do this by changing the game. By expanding the role of the position and what you can add to it, you can become the first impression in the minds of interviewers, even though you are not the first to interview.

When you raise the bar and redefine what qualities and experiences are necessary for the position, you recreate the whole playing field. You now become the new first impression.

## TUESDAY OR THURSDAY

Ideally, you want to interview on Tuesday or Thursday. Mondays are bad because Mondays often are spent getting organized and planning for the week. Wednesdays are sometimes unpleasant because people like to take a mid-week break, and it is a typical day for internal meetings. Fridays are poor because everyone is focused on the weekend.

### Best time to interview 9:30 am - 10:30 am
### Worst time to interview 1:00 pm - 2:30 pm

If possible, you should schedule your interview in the morning, about 9:30 am. People are usually more alert in the morning and have not had enough time to have a bad day. It is usually after 10:30 am when problems and disruptions start. You should not interview before 9:30 am because people take a good hour to get through the morning mail and paperwork, and to get their bearings. By 9:30 am, however, the coffee has kicked in and interviewers will be ready for you.

Try not to interview too late in the morning. After 11:00 am, interviewers will start to get hungry and will be thinking more about lunch than your skills for the job.

The absolute worst time to interview is right after lunch. Neither you nor the interviewer will be alert and the interview will not go well.

When I interviewed candidates, I hated that first interview after lunch. Inevitably, I would become sleepy. This always caused me considerable distraction. The person I was interviewing had to be extremely good to make a big impression on me.

After lunch, most people need a good hour to fully digest their meal and wake up. If you must interview in the afternoon, try to schedule it between 2:30 pm and 3:30 pm.

After 3:30 pm, interviewers will be thinking more about going home than about your job credentials. For me, the last interview of the day was always the pits because, at that point, my voice was dead and I was tired of asking the same questions over and over again. I have yet to participate in a good interview at the end of the day.

# THE BEST TIMES TO INTERVIEW

## CHECKLIST SUMMARY

✔ Try to be the FIRST person to INTERVIEW

✔ If you can't be FIRST, RAISE the BAR so you CREATE a NEW FIRST IMPRESSION

✔ TUESDAYS and THURSDAYS are the BEST days to INTERVIEW

✔ 9:30 am – 10:30 am is the BEST MORNING time to INTERVIEW

✔ 2:30 pm – 3:30 pm is the BEST AFTERNOON time to INTERVIEW

"When you raise the bar and redefine what qualities and experiences are necessary for the position, you recreate the whole playing field. You now become the new first impression."

# BONUS #vi

## PROPER INTERVIEWING ETIQUETTE

- **No Eating, Drinking or Smoking**
- **Listen, Listen, Listen**
- **Interviewing "Do's" and "Don'ts"**

In everyday life, it is often the little things that can make or break a situation. Interviewing is no different. The tips that I am going to give you in this section should not be taken lightly.

## NO EATING, DRINKING OR SMOKING

First of all, when interviewing, do not drink, eat or chew gum. Not only is this unprofessional, but it could annoy interviewers. I have seen people chew gum during an interview like a cow chomping on grass. All I could think of is watching the mouth go up and down, up and down. What was that they were saying? Who cares?

Also, interviewers might offer you a soft drink, coffee or water. What should you do? I recommend that you politely turn down the offer. I say this for two reasons. First, having a beverage gives you one more thing to worry about. You start thinking more about the drink than the interview. Second, a beverage gives you a great target to knock over. If you are like me, and use hand gestures when you speak, you could spill a hot cup of coffee into the interviewer's lap—not a good idea!

Finally, you should never smoke during an interview. Smoking can inhibit your concentration and also irritate interviewers. Even if an interviewer smokes, DO NOT follow suit. Politely decline a cigarette if offered.

## LISTEN, LISTEN, LISTEN

As humans, you were created with two ears and one mouth for a reason. You should listen twice as much as you talk. Quite often, people hear but do not listen. Do not do this during the interview. Pay attention and keep good eye contact. If you are well prepared, your mind will not need to wander while the other person is talking.

By listening carefully, you will be able to respond more intelligently to statements and questions.

Also, never interrupt interviewers! Often, you will be so excited that you will want to respond before interviewers finish with what they have to say. If you do this, interviewers will get upset and eventually start to tune you out when you talk.

## INTERVIEWING "DON'TS"

a) Don't share proprietary information about your existing employer. You will lose all credibility.

b) Don't ramble on. Be short, concise and to the point. An interviewer's time is valuable and you don't want to waste it. Make sure that before you say something, you answer in your mind, "So what?" If you were the interviewer, would you care about what you are going to say? If the answer to "So what?" is positive, then go ahead. However, if you ask "So what?" and you don't have a good response, then don't say it.

c) Don't ever disparage your current company. Be positive when stating why you are leaving. Give your current boss and employer high praises. Then, shift the focus to the fact that you are ready for the next challenge.

d) Don't tell interviewers what you are currently earning. If you mention how much you are currently making, you have just capped your potential offer. By not mentioning current compensation, you place yourself in a much better bargaining position.

e) Don't show up late to the interview. That will immediately leave a bad taste in the interviewer's mouth, and you most likely will be rejected just because of that.

# INTERVIEWING "DO'S"—FINAL TIPS

a) Sit down only when asked.

b) Cross your legs only if the interviewer does.

c) Eat lightly before the interview and at least an hour in advance. You can celebrate with a good meal after the interview.

d) Brush your teeth and use mouthwash before the interview. Bring breath mints with you.

e) Ask to take notes if you wish.

f) Have a professional greeting on your answering machine or voicemail. Do not use a funny saying or play rock music on your recording. I once had an interviewer tell me to change my recording because it was not professional. Can you imagine how that made me feel? Needless to say, even to this day, I have a professional recording on my voicemail.

g) Use voicemail instead of an answering machine. Voicemail is typically less than $10 a month and provided by your local phone carrier. I prefer voicemail to an answering machine because it can pick up if you are not home, or even if you are on the other line. Imagine if you have call waiting and one company calls you while you are on the phone with another. You don't want to be rude and take the call waiting. With voicemail, you can just let the call waiting go to voicemail and return their call when you get off the phone. Also, voicemail is far more reliable than answering machines. You don't have to worry about power outages or tapes running out. And finally, voicemail is more professional.

h) If you are currently employed, try to save up at least three months of living expenses before you begin your job hunt. This is ideal because it takes any financial pressure off you and allows you to interview at the top of your game. Ideally, the best time to look for another job is while you are still employed and have plenty of savings in the bank. But if you don't have that luxury, try to save as much money as possible and cut down on your expenses during the process.

i) After each interview, grade yourself. Ask yourself what you did well on and where you could have improved. Write down notes on these areas so you can continually improve on your interviewing techniques.

j) Smile and have fun!

# PROPER INTERVIEWING ETIQUETTE

## CHECKLIST SUMMARY

✔ NO Eating, Drinking or SMOKING

✔ Listen, Listen, LISTEN

✔ Tell only POSITION-RELEVANT INFORMATION

✔ Be Positive and DON'T DISPARAGE your current EMPLOYER

✔ Use VOICEMAIL and have a PROFESSIONAL GREETING

✔ SMILE and HAVE FUN

**"You have two ears and one mouth for a reason. Listen . . . Listen . . . Listen!"**

# BONUS #vii

## LEGALITIES OF INTERVIEWING

- **Inappropriate Topics**
- **EEOC Perspective**

**W**hen it comes to interviewing, hopefully you will not have to deal with any legal issues. But, no book on job hunting would be complete without giving you an overview of your rights. That said, I would like to preface this chapter by saying that I am not a lawyer and much of what I will say can be left up to interpretation. This is for information purposes only and shall not be construed as formal legal advice. To find out exactly what your rights are, you should refer to a lawyer or a book specifically written on the topic.

With that disclaimer made, I want to give you an idea of the topics and questions that are off limits to interviewers. In an interview, it is important for interviewers to keep the questions to relevant work-related history. Very personal topics (i.e. age, religion, etc.) have no relevance in an interview. In fact, many of the topics below are illegal to discuss in the interview setting.

What follows are topics that you should not have to discuss during an interview.

## INAPPROPRIATE TOPICS

> ❏ **Political Affiliation**
> ❏ **National Origin and/or Citizenship**
> ❏ **Sexual Preference**

❏ **Medical History**

❏ **Physiological or Psychological Disorders**

❏ **Economic Status**

Interviewers are not allowed to ask a man questions they would not ask a woman, or vice versa. In addition, interviewers cannot ask any question of a minority that they would not ask of a non-minority.

Unfortunately, there are interviewers who have unlawfully used their position for personal gain. You should know what your rights are, especially when it comes to harassment.

## EEOC PERSPECTIVE

If you want further information on what your rights are, you can contact the Equal Employment Opportunity Commission (EEOC). The EEOC is an U.S. government commission that promotes and enforces equal opportunity in the workplace. The EEOC has a web site that is very helpful and goes into tremendous detail about your rights as an individual in the labor force. You can reach this web site by going to www.eeoc.gov.

If you are asked questions that you feel are not appropriate, or are in a situation where harassment is present, my best advice is to politely state that you would like to keep the interview to relevant topics and not discuss personal aspects. If the situation gets worse, your best bet is to end the interview. Most likely, if people like this are managing at the company, you don't want to work there. Depending of the severity of the situation, you may want to obtain the advice of legal counsel.

You have a right to an open and fair interview, where you are judged on your merits, not on your gender, beliefs and other non-relevant personal information.

# LEGALITIES OF INTERVIEWING

## CHECKLIST SUMMARY

✔ **KNOW your RIGHTS**

✔ **Don't answer INAPPROPRIATE QUESTIONS**

✔ **Go to WWW.EEOC.GOV for EXACT DETAILS on your RIGHTS**

✔ **If you are asked an inappropriate question, POLITELY state that you would like to keep the INTERVIEW focused on POSITION— RELEVANT INFORMATION**

**"You have a right to an open and fair interview, where you are judged on your merits, not on your gender, beliefs and other non-relevant personal information."**

# SUMMARY

**A**re you smiling and having fun yet? You should be. If you follow the advice given in this book, you will get the job you want. Get psyched! You are among the select few who can conquer any challenge presented to you in an interview. Just the fact that you took the time to read this book and improve your skills means that you are a WINNER!

### Only the Cream of the Crop
### Will Have Completed This Book!

By investing the time you have just invested in yourself, you will succeed. Also, hang on to this book for future reference. Keep the book with you in your car. I have included some pages in the back of this book so you can take notes during your job hunt. Review your notes before and after the interview and you will have fantastic results.

### Hunting for a Job Is Nothing More Than a Game!
### Be prepared and confident.
### Believe That You are #1 and Have FUN!

At this time, I would like to thank you for investing your hard-earned time and money in this book. I wish you wonderful success in your job hunting as well as in your personal life. It has been a tremendous honor to be able to share these moments with you.

### Now . . . Go Out and Get the Job of Your Dreams!

# GOOD LUCK AND GOOD INTERVIEWING!

# PERSONAL JOB INTERVIEWING JOURNAL

Date: _____

"Ideal Job" Mission Statement:_____

_____

_____

Job Hunting Notes: _____

_____

_____

_____

_____

_____

_____

_____

_____

_____

_____

_____

# PERSONAL JOB INTERVIEWING JOURNAL

Date: _____

"Ideal Job" Mission Statement:_____

_____

_____

Job Hunting Notes: _____

_____

_____

_____

_____

_____

_____

_____

_____

_____

_____

_____

_____

_____

_____

# PERSONAL JOB INTERVIEWING JOURNAL

Date: _____

"Ideal Job" Mission Statement: _____
_____
_____

Job Hunting Notes: _____
_____
_____

_____
_____

_____
_____

_____
_____

_____
_____

# OTHER NOTES

# INDEX

# B

# C

# I

# J

## N

# Q

# R

## S

# Y

# X

# Z

# SPEAK WITH THE AUTHOR

## $A$re you interested in . . .?

✔ A Personal Interview Coach

✔ Feedback on a Possible Career Change

✔ Having an Expert Review Your Resume

✔ Increasing Your Motivation and Staying
   at the Top of Your Game

✔ Getting Customized Assistance on Your Job Hunt

✔ Feeling Better About Yourself

FOR A NOMINAL FEE, YOU CAN SPEAK WITH THE AUTHOR OF THIS BOOK
TODD BERMONT AND HAVE YOUR VERY OWN PERSONAL CAREER COACH!
FOR MORE INFORMATION ON CAREER COACHING AND OTHER SERVICES
PLEASE REFER TO WWW.BERMONT.COM OR CALL **(888) 894-6400.**

# PUT YOUR JOB HUNT ON THE FAST TRACK . . . SPECIAL OFFERS!!!

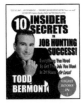

## 10 INSIDER SECRETS TO JOB HUNTING SUCCESS!

Share this powerful book with your friends and family! Whether graduating from college or having years of work experience, this book will help any job hunter succeed!

| | | |
|---|---|---|
| **Single Book:** | ...................... | $16.95 |
| **Shipping/Handling Per Book** | ................... | $2.75 |

*Order 5 or More and Save 10%*

## The Secret To Developing Instant Rapport Even If You Don't Know How To Tell A Joke!

This tape gives you eight easy strategies to unlock your hidden charisma so you can create instant rapport with anyone you meet over the phone or in person. Ideal for job interviewing! You'll learn how to turn on your "magnetic energy" for winning results. You'll find this information also useful in business meetings and social gatherings.

| | | |
|---|---|---|
| **Single Audiocassette Tape:** | ................... | $15.95 |
| **Shipping/Handling Per Tape** | ................... | $2.75 |

*Save 10% . . . Buy Tape + Book*

## 10 INSIDER SECRETS... Interview Coaching Special!

This personalized coaching session will give you the winning edge you need going into your job hunt! Get One Hour of Interview Coaching from your author, Todd Bermont. During this hour, Todd will review your resume, motivate you, educate you, answer your career questions, and get you psyched and prepared for your job hunt! Special Offer—50% discount for readers of 10 Insider Secrets To Job Hunting Success!

**One-Hour Interview Coaching Special:** ~~$250~~ ........... $125     *Save 50%!*

All products are available at special quantity discounts for bulk purchases for sales promotions, premiums, fund-raising, corporate use or educational use. Special books or book excerpts also can be created to fit specific needs.

**For details, write 10 Step Publications at info@10StepPublications.com or call (888) 894-6400.**

---

Payable in US funds only. Postage and handling: US $2.75 per book and tape, International $5 per book and tape. We accept Visa, MC, checks ($15.00 fee for returned checks) and money orders. No Cash / COD. Call (888) 894-6400, fax (312) 751-8093 or mail your orders to: 10 Step Publications, Attn: Todd Bermont,1151 N. State Pkwy #253, Chicago, IL 60610

### YES, I CAN'T WAIT TO LAND MY IDEAL JOB! PLEASE RUSH THE FOLLOWING ORDER!

| ITEM | UNIT PRICE | SPECIAL OFFER | QUANTITY | TOTAL |
|---|---|---|---|---|
| **Job Hunting Book** | $ 16.95 | $15.25 (5 or More) | _____ | $_____ |
| **Rapport Building Tape** | $ 15.95 | $29.95 (Book+Tape) | _____ | $_____ |
| **Interview Coaching** | $ ~~250~~ | $125 (Book Special) | _____ | $_____ |

Bill to: _____     Subtotal: $_____

Address: _____     US Shipping/Handling: $_____

City: _____ ST_____ Zip_____     Total Amount Due: $_____

Bill my credit card #: _____     **expiration date:** _____ Visa_____ MC_____

**Signature:** _____

Ship to (if different then bill to): _____

Address: _____

City: _____ ST_____ Zip_____

**This offer is subject to change without notice.**

# ABOUT THE AUTHOR

## TODD BERMONT

Todd Bermont is president and founder of 10 Step Corporation, a firm specializing in motivational speaking, publishing, sales training, and executive coaching. Bermont graduated with Honors from the University of Illinois.

Prior to founding 10 Step Corporation, Bermont worked in executive management and corporate sales at some of the world's leading corporations including Royal Dutch Shell Corporation, NCR Corporation, IBM Corporation and American Power Conversion Corporation.

Bermont has worked in over twenty countries, with more than half of the Fortune 500. As part of his goal to give back to the community, Bermont also has volunteered his time teaching job hunting skills to inner-city high school students. Throughout his career, Bermont has helped thousands of people across the globe succeed in their careers.